HARRY P PLACES

BOOK TWO

OWLs: OXFORD WIZARDING LOCATIONS

A Novel Holiday Travel Guidebook

By CD Miller

Harry Potter Places BOOK TWO
OWLs: Oxford Wizarding Locations
A Novel Holiday Travel Guidebook

by CD Miller

Published by:
A Novel Holiday Travel Guidebooks
16614 226th Street
Ashland, NE 68003
http://www.anovelholiday.com

The publisher and author(s) of *Harry Potter Places* Book Two have taken great care to ensure that all information provided is correct and accurate at the time of manuscript submission. However, errors and omissions—whether typographical, clerical or otherwise—do sometimes occur, and may occur anywhere within the body of this publication.

Changes in real-life site information will inevitably occur. As aptly stated by the Internationally-renown travel guidebook author, **Rick Steves**: "Guidebooks begin to yellow even before they're printed." This rule holds true for eBooks, as well.

Users of any *Harry Potter Places* travel guidebook are advised to access the Internet links provided within each Site entry in order to obtain the most up-to-date information during the planning of your UK Potter holiday. For instance, the ticket and entry fees cited are those that were in effect during our last pass at researching each site.

Currency equivalents are offered only to provide an *approximate idea* of what British Pounds (£) equals in US Dollars ($). Currency exchange rates change daily. Check current foreign exchange rates by using a free Internet currency converter such as the one offered by **Oanda**:
http://www.oanda.com/currency/converter/

The publisher and author(s) of *Harry Potter Places* travel guidebooks hereby disclaim any liability to any party for loss, injury, or damage incurred as a direct or indirect consequence of errors, omissions, or post-manuscript-submission information changes, whether such errors, omissions, or changes result from negligence, accident, or any other cause.

Copyright © 2012 by Charly D Miller
A Novel Holiday Travel Guidebooks Publishing Company
Printed in the United States of America
ISBN 978-1-938285-17-2

Publisher's Cataloging-in-Publication Data
Miller, Charly D, 1956 -
Harry Potter Places Book Two (Color)—OWLs: Oxford Wizarding Locations
    p. cm.
    includes index
    ISBN 978-1-938285-17-2 (softbound) $25.99
    1. Travel Guides—United Kingdom—.
I. Title.
DA650.H75 M460 2012

DISCLAIMERS

J.K. Rowling's *Harry Potter* books are so popular, that an amazing number of **unauthorized** *Harry Potter* guidebooks have been published over the years.
http://harrypotter.wikia.com/wiki/List_of_Harry_Potter_unofficial_guidebooks

In order to avoid the threat of litigation related to copyright or trademark infringement, all unauthorized *Harry Potter* guidebooks publish at least one **Disclaimer**. Below are the **several** important *Harry Potter Places* Disclaimers.

An Unauthorized *Harry Potter* Travel Guidebook

Harry Potter Places Book Two [hereinafter referred to as **HPP Book Two**] is not authorized, approved, endorsed, nor licensed by J.K. Rowling [hereinafter referred to as **JKR**], Warner Bros. Entertainment, Inc. [hereinafter referred to as **WB Inc**], the Scholastic Corporation, Raincoast Books, Bloomsbury Publishing Plc., nor by any other persons, entities, corporations or companies claiming a proprietary interest in the *Harry Potter* books, movies, or related merchandise.

HPP Book Two is not officially associated with the seven *Harry Potter* novels written and copyrighted by JKR. Nor is HPP Book Two in any way officially associated with the eight *Harry Potter* movies produced and trade-marked by WB Inc.

The Purpose of Book Two

HPP Book Two is written solely for the purpose of providing an historical review of, and directions for finding, the **real-life** Oxford and nearby-Oxford locations that:
- Were mentioned within one or more of the *Harry Potter* novels.
- Are sites where Harry Potter filming took place.
- Significantly influenced the design of studio sets built for filming one or more of the *Harry Potter* movies.

HP-Associated Names, Places, Titles or Terminology

HPP Book Two does not claim, nor does it intend to imply, ownership of, or proprietary rights to, any of the fictional character or place names mentioned within JKR's *Harry Potter* novels, nor any of the titles or terminology used or created by JKR within her books or within the movies made thereof.

More information about Potter and Potterlike terminology found within HPP Book Two is provided in the **Prior Incantato** section.

Publication of *Harry Potter* Movie Screenshots

Screenshots are split-second still photos captured from a movie. Each of the four (4) HPP Book Two Potter Site entries include one or more small movie screenshots. The sole purpose of including them is to enhance the experience of *Harry Potter* fans [**Potterites**] who visit a real-life film site, or a real-life place that strongly influenced movie studio set design. By having one or more screenshots to observe while visiting, Potterites are better able to recognize the specific areas where filming occurred, and are armed with a guide important to assuming positions similar to that of the actors in the scene(s) filmed at the site when snapping their personal photographs.

To be an effective site identification and photography guide, however, *Harry Potter* movie screenshots had to be substantially *altered* in a variety of ways so that the site location's **background** could more easily be recognized.

All eight *Harry Potter* films were produced and trademarked by WB Inc. HPP Book Two does not claim, nor does it intend to imply, ownership of, or proprietary rights to, any portions of the *Harry Potter* movies. The caption of every screenshot and screenshot segment that appears within HPP should read "™©WB Inc." Because this info is given here, we instead have captioned HPP screenshots with identification of the movie from which it was captured.

Use of Google Maps UK Images to Create Potter Maps

In order to assist visiting Potterites to find multiple filming locations within one Site (such as the Knight Bus Pickup Playground, or the Ministry of Magic Area), a few **Potter Maps** were created for *Harry Potter Places* Book Two.

When using Google Maps UK images to create Potter Maps, HPP Book Two authors strictly adhered to the *Google Maps and Google Earth Content Rules & Guidelines*, and appropriately attributed Google with credit for the full-sized Potter Map included within a Supplementum PDF posted on the Internet, as well as for any thumbnail-sized Potter Map images published within the travel guidebook.

HPP Book Two does not claim, nor does it intend to imply, ownership of, or proprietary rights to, any of the Google Maps UK images used within the travel guidebook or the Supplementum PDFs posted on HarryPotter-Places. com.

Author vs Authors of *Harry Potter Places*

The **A Novel Holiday** travel guidebook publishing company concept was solely conceived by Ms. Charly D Miller in 2007, as was the concept of the first series of A Novel Holiday (**ANH**) travel guidebooks, *Harry Potter Places*. However, during the researching and writing of HPP travel guidebooks (as well as during design of the ANH and HPP websites), Ms. Miller was so generously assisted by other individuals, that she feels unworthy of claiming sole credit for authoring the text's or websites' content. Thus, **plural terms**—such as, "authors" … "we" … "our"—are used throughout the HPP travel guidebooks, as well as throughout the ANH and HPP websites, when referring to the writers or creators of same.

However, for all legal purposes, every A Novel Holiday *Harry Potter Places* travel guidebook was solely written and published by CD Miller. She, alone, is responsible for all the content ultimately published within any eBook or print versions of the HPP travel guidebooks, as well as all the content posted on ANH and HPP websites.

Ms. Charly D Miller hereby avows and affirms that any and all other individuals who participated in or contributed to the researching, writing, or publication of *Harry Potter Places* travel guidebooks and associated websites, are **indemnified and held harmless** from and against: any and all demands, claims, and damages to persons or property, losses and liabilities, including attorney's fees arising out of or caused by any form of litigation brought against the A Novel Holiday *Harry Potter Places* travel guidebooks or websites.

CREDITS AND ACKNOWLEDGMENTS

Thank you, Tara and Wolfgang!

The two most generous and dedicated Contributing *Harry Potter Places* Researchers are Ms. Tara Bellers of the US, and Mr. Wolfgang Mletzko of Germany.

Tara Bellers traveled from the US to the UK on three different occasions between 2009 and 2011. During each of those trips, she voluntarily spent personal time investigating answers to Potter Place questions that couldn't be found on the Internet. In addition to snapping location pix for us, Tara discovered and reported info important to enhancing other Potterites' enjoyment of a similar visit.

When not traveling, Tara continued to significantly contribute to this project. While at home, she independently performed hundreds of hours of Internet research, leading to the discovery of several important Potter Places we might have missed. Thanks to Tara, Potterites will have no trouble finding even the most obscure UK Potter Places.

Wolfgang Mletzko began visiting UK Potter Places long before A Novel Holiday travel guidebooks (let alone *Harry Potter Places*) were even a concept. Since 2002, Wolfgang has performed several well-researched UK Potter treks, and always has freely-posted his marvelous photos and Potter travel tips on his website—which is how we found him!
http://www.bdyg.homepage.t-online.de/index.html

If you can't read German, go to **Google's Translation** website and paste-in Wolfgang's website address.
http://translate.google.com/

Photo Credits

Beneath each photograph in *Harry Potter Places* is the name of the person who snapped the pic. With few exceptions, permission for using these photos was granted free of charge. Some photos were obtained from **Wikipedia** or **Wikimedia**, where they were posted by photographers who generously offered the freedom of their commercial re-use.

Art Credit

The *Harry Potter Places* **Coat of Arms**—an emblem seen on the title page of every *Harry Potter Places* Supplementum and Portkey PDF, as well as in the Banner atop each HarryPotterPlaces.com webpage—was designed by two terrifically talented graphic artists, **Karen Stoehr** and **Ben Dale**. They also created our three site ratings icons. Thank you both, so very much, for all your work!

http://www.coroflot.com/kstoehr
http://bendale.daportfolio.com/

OWLs Map Credit

Potterites have **Linda Barna of Lincoln, Nebraska**, to thank for the crisp and clear quality of the OWLs Map. Our original version was horrible!

Book Cover Credits

DC Carson created all five of the original 2012 HPP Book Covers—free of charge! Were it not for her, the HPP books and website would not have had images to use while CD Miller was still broke.

All photos used for the HPP Book Covers were snapped by **Ms. Tara Bellers**.

Acknowledgments

From the Author, CD Miller
To Ms. Carson

I am more grateful to Ms. Carson than mere words can possibly convey.

Dina has helped me with this project from the very beginning—for more than three years—entirely free of charge! These guidebooks would be *krappe* were it not for Dina's incredible writing talent and editing instruction, as well as her invaluable assistance with getting the eBook and print versions published. Dina also was vitally important to the design of the A Novel Holiday and *Harry Potter Places* websites.

My fondest wish is to someday be able to reciprocate, and help her as significantly as she's helped me. Unfortunately, I cannot imagine what *I* could ever do that Dina can't do better! Thankfully, I anticipate being able to *financially* reward her for all her work very soon.

Then, there's Tara Bellers

I couldn't afford to visit the UK more than *once*—a measly 2 weeks in 2008—while initially working on the *Harry Potter Places* project. Thus, the information offered in all HPP books would be terrifically incomplete were it not for Tara's **voluntary** UK Potter Place site research and photography, as well as the Internet research she continues to freely perform. In addition to that, Tara took me to the *Wizarding World of Harry Potter* in Orlando, Florida, in 2010!

I'll *never* be able to adequately thank Tara for all her generosity and assistance. But, perhaps I'll soon be able to reward her by taking her on an all-expenses-paid UK trip!

As for my Personal Friends

Susan and Bob, Jamie, Janet, Chet, Sandy, Leeenda and Mike ... these are just a *few* of the scores of people I need to thank!

I was broke and homeless. (Much like JKR was while writing *Sorcerer's Stone*, oddly enough.) Yet, each of my friends contributed—in their own way—to ensure that I had a place to live, and the means for living comfortably, during the several years it took me to complete my first HPP travel guidebooks. You guys have no idea how much I've appreciated your help. I swear that, someday, I'll find a way of repaying you.

Lastly, to Drew and Annabeth, Auntie Dot and Uncle Itchy

Bless You for always believing in me!

TABLE OF CONTENTS

Chapter 1—PRIOR INCANTATO (Introduction)

Chapter 2—LUMOS BRITANNIA

Chapter 3—LUMOS OXFORD

Chapter 4—SPECIALIS REVELIO OXFORD

Chapter 5—AMBULATUS OXFORD

POTTER PLACES IN OXFORD

Please Note: Our Site numbers continue from *Harry Potter Places* Book One—London and London Side-Along Apparations.

PRIOR INCANTATO

Welcome to the **A Novel Holiday** travel guidebook, *Harry Potter Places* **Book 2—OWLs: Oxford Wizarding Locations**, the second of five guidebooks designed to help *Harry Potter* Fans (**Potterites**) visit places found in the United Kingdom of Great Britain (the **UK**) that are associated with the *Harry Potter* Universe (the **Potterverse**). In the Potterverse, you'll find:

- Real-life places mentioned within J.K. Rowling's *Harry Potter* novels.
- Real-life locations where *Harry Potter* movie filming took place.
- Real-life sites that significantly influenced *Harry Potter* movie studio set design.

The **Prior Incantato** section is the *Harry Potter Places* Travel Guidebook **Introduction.** As such, it contains important explanations of the symbols and terminology found within each of the five *Harry Potter Places* (**HPP**) travel guidebooks.

Harry Potter Places Portkeys

To assist Potterites using eBook-reading devices that don't have a web browser—devices from which you cannot apparate—or Potterites using a printed HPP travel guidebook, we've created **HPP Portkeys**: Internet-posted PDFs containing all the Internet resource links provided in each section of every HPP book.

Go to **HarryPotterPlaces.com.** Click on the link for **Book Two**, then click on the **Supplementums** link. There you can access the Portkeys.

Harry Potter Places Ratings Icon Guide

It took more than three years of research, but we managed to find *sixty-eight* **(68) Potter Places in the UK**—specifically on the island of Great Britain. However, not all of these sites are places every Potterite will enjoy. Thus, we assessed each for their reasonable importance to an average Potterite's UK holiday, and created icons that provide an *at-a-glance* recognition of their rating.

The **Great Site** icon indicates a Potter Place you don't want to miss. These are important sites mentioned in the books, or film locations readily recognized in real-life.

The **Might Be Fun** icon identifies places some Potterites might find disinteresting, *or* unworthy of the inconvenience required to reach them. Each Might-Be-Fun Site's entry explains why it received that rating.

The **Skip It** icon is assigned to places we strongly suggest you *avoid* visiting, and the Site's entry explains why. Although we provide SatNav/GPS coordinates and/or addresses for Skip-It-rated sites, we do not provide directions for finding them, nor are Skip-It sites included in *any* of the suggested *Harry Potter Places* itineraries. Potterites divinely inspired to visit any Skip-It site should investigate the location using the information provided in its Site entry, then create their own itineraries.

The Potterite Prime Directive

To *POLITELY* Go Where Potterites Need to Go
— without **PERTURBING** anybody —
So That Other Potterites Can *Continue*
to ENJOY GOING THERE!

It is vitally important that all Potterites be as polite as possible when visiting *any* Potter Place. This rule is even more important when visiting a Site situated within a **private Muggle neighborhood**. It only takes *one* noisy or disrespectful fan to ruin the reception experienced by *all* Potterites who visit thereafter. Please be the very best **Potterite Ambassador** you can possibly be, everywhere you go.

Terminology Used within *Harry Potter Places*

Like any other author of fiction, J.K. Rowling (**JKR**) exercised *artistic license* when selecting or creating names, phrases, and terms for her Potterverse. Most often, she borrowed from Latin and Greek languages or mythologies. Occasionally, JKR's Potterverse terminology was influenced by other languages, such as French, Irish, Italian—even Arabic. Below are links to two resources that comprehensively discus the origin of Potterverse names, phrases, and terms.
http://www.harrypotterfanzone.com/word-origins/
http://www.languagerealm.com/hplang/harrypotterlanguage.php

JKR also often used words that *predate* her creation of the Potterverse, such as Witch, Wizard, broomstick, and the like. Sometimes, JKR altered the previously-popular meaning of the words she used. For instance, *Time Magazine* reported in 1931 that "Muggle" was one of several slang names for a **marijuana cigarette**.
http://www.time.com/time/magazine/article/0,9171,742157,00.html

The authors of *Harry Potter Places* have similarly exercised artistic license when using Potterverse terminology within our travel guidebooks. Some names, phrases, and terms used within HPP have the same meaning as they do in the Potterverse. Others have been redefined.

For example: **Prior Incantato** is a Potterverse incantation spoken to reveal the last spell performed by a wand. JKR created this phrase from the Latin word, *prior*, meaning former or previous, in combination with *incanto*, meaning "to enchant," or *incantate*, meaning "to speak a spell." However, in the *Harry Potter Places* travel guidebooks, Prior Incantato is the title of each books' **Introduction**.

Potterverse names, phrases, and terms found within *Harry Potter Places* that may have been independently-created by J.K. Rowling are used only for the purpose of enhancing Potterites' enjoyment of the travel guidebook. The authors of *Harry Potter Places* do not claim, nor intend to imply, ownership of, or proprietary rights to, any terminology found exclusively within *Harry Potter* books.

Some Potterverse—and Potterlike—Terms Used

Ambulatus

Although **Ambulatus** *sounds* Potterlike, it isn't found anywhere within JKR's Potterverse. Ambulate is an English word derived from Latin origins, and means, "to walk from place to place" or "move about." The Latin word for navigated, traveled, or traversed, is *ambulatus*. Ambulatus is used in the title of *Harry Potter Places* sections that provide directions for walking or traveling about within the cities of Oxford and Edinburgh. (London's between-Potter-Places travel directions are found at the end of each site entry.)

Huffandpuff

Hufflepuff is one of the four Houses of Hogwarts School of Witchcraft and Wizardry. While **Huffandpuff** sounds like Hufflepuff, it is a term created by *Harry Potter Places* authors for use as the title of any particularly arduous itinerary or walking route—indicating that you may be *huffing and puffing* when you reach the end!

Lumos

In the Potterverse, Lumos is the spell-word uttered to cause a wand to emit light from its tip. Lumos is related to *lumen*, a Latin word for light. In *Harry Potter Places*, **Lumos** is used in the title of sections that *shed a light on* a particular location, providing Potter- and Non-Potter-related information important to planning or enjoying your trek to that place.

Muggle

Every Potterite knows the Potterverse definition of a Muggle. In *Harry Potter Places*, **Muggle** is a term used when referring to any Non-Potterites one might encounter while visiting a Potter place, particularly *indigenous* Non-Potterites—those who live in the private neighborhoods that Potterites may be visiting.

NEWTs

NEWTs is a Potterverse acronym for the **Nastily Exhausting Wizarding Tests** that Hogwarts' students must pass at the end of their seventh year of school. In *Harry Potter Places*, however, **NEWTs** refers to **Northeastern England Wizarding Treks**, Potter Places that can be visited in Northeastern England.

OWLs

In the Potterverse, Hogwarts' students are subjected to **OWLs—Ordinary Wizarding Level** examinations—at the end of their fifth year of school. In *Harry Potter Places*, **OWLs** stands for **Oxford Wizarding Locations**, Potter Places found in the city of Oxford.

Parseltongue Pointers

Parseltongue is the Potterverse language spoken by a Parselmouth—someone who can communicate with snakes. In *Harry Potter Places*, **Parseltongue Pointers** are guides to correctly pronouncing place names associated with UK Potter Sites.

Specialis Revelio

A Potterverse spell invoked to reveal the ingredients of a potion or the enchantments placed upon an object, **Specialis Revelio** is a phrase created from the Latin terms *specialis*, meaning special, and *revelo*, meaning "to unveil." In *Harry Potter Places*, **Specialis Revelio** is used as the title of a section that reveals special information about visiting a particular location—including suggested itineraries.

Supplementum(s)

Another term that *sounds* Potterlike, but isn't found anywhere within JKR's Potterverse, **Supplementum** is a *Harry Potter Places* term for am Internet-posted PDF that contains extra information related to an individual Potter place. HPP Supplementums are intended to enrich a Potterite's visit to the Site they are associated with.

Please Note: Although it is more grammatically-correct to consider **Supplementum** as *both* the singular and plural version of this term, the authors of *Harry Potter Places* have elected to use **Supplementums** as the plural form of Supplementum.

Philosopher's Stone vs Sorcerer's Stone

There are a number of unconfirmed theories as to why the title of J.K. Rowling's first book, **Harry Potter and the Philosopher's Stone**, was changed to **Harry Potter and the Sorcerer's Stone** for release in the USA and elsewhere. Because the authors of *Harry Potter Places* live in the USA, *Sorcerer's Stone* is used whenever we refer to the first *Harry Potter* book and movie.

We intend no disrespect to JKR—nor to Potterites living in the UK, Canada, or Australia (countries where both the book and movie are called, *Philosopher's Stone*)—by electing to use *Sorcerer's Stone* when referring to the first *Harry Potter* book and movie.

LUMOS BRITANNIA

Lumos Britannia provides general tips for Potterites planning a visit to **the United Kingdom of Great Britain**—aka **Britannia**, aka **the UK**.

UK Travel Guidebooks

Consider purchasing one or more Non-Potter (Muggle) UK travel guidebooks related to the areas where you'll be Pottering. If your holiday is solely Potter-centric, a UK Muggle travel guidebook is *not* necessary— *Harry Potter Places* will take care of you. However, Potterites also interested in visiting Non-Potter UK places will benefit from buying one *or more* Muggle travel guidebooks.

The *Harry Potter Places* Travel Store offers links to many of the Travel Guidebooks mentioned below, including several eBook versions.

HPP Recommends Rick Steves' Guidebooks
http://www.ricksteves.com

Rick Steves has been researching and writing truly excellent travel guidebooks for over 20 years, and he publishes three frequently-updated UK guides for the places you might be traveling to. Potterites only visiting London should buy *Rick Steves' London*. If you'll be visiting London and Oxford (and/or other places in England), purchase *Rick Steves' England*. If you'll be visiting England, Wales, *and* Scotland, buy *Rick Steves' Great Britain*.

Other Popular UK Muggle Travel Guidebook Companies
Fodor's Travel Guides
http://www.fodors.com

Frommer's Travel Guides
http://www.frommers.com/

Lonely Planet Guides
http://www.lonelyplanet.com/

Rough Guides
http://www.roughguides.com/

FREE UK Travel Tips Available on the Internet

Here are our favorites.

Rick Steves' Website

Whether or not you purchase a Rick Steves travel guidebook, his website offers free access to a ton of terrific European travel tip articles: packing, safety issues, health information, communicating [phone info], money matters, and other important subjects.
http://www.ricksteves.com/plan/tips/tips_menu.htm

Steves' Website also offers free travel tip articles for visiting London, England, Wales, Edinburgh, and Scotland.
http://www.ricksteves.com/plan/destinations/britain/brit_menu.htm

Reid Bramblett's Website
http://www.reidsguides.com/

In 1997, travel expert and guidebook author Reid Bramblett began what has become one of the most helpful travel planning websites on the Internet.

> "ReidsGuides.com is focused on European trip planning, with emphasis on money-saving tips and alternatives to traditional travel techniques, such as lodging options beyond hotels, no-frills airlines, short-term car leases, and sightseeing for free."

Bramblett also offers free articles about all the **traditional** UK trip planning subjects. But, he excels at making complicated money issues easy to understand. *All* of Bramblett's money articles are valuable when planning a UK trip, particularly the ones about changing money, using credit cards, and traveler's checks.

> "Here's how to get money during your [UK] travels, strategies for getting the best deals on exchange rates, how to avoid scams and rip-offs, and ways to save money every step of the way on your vacation."

http://www.reidsguides.com/t_mo/t_mo_money.html

Visit Travel Websites Related to Planning a UK Holiday

US Department of State, Bureau of Consular Affairs' Website
http://travel.state.gov/travel/cis_pa_tw/cis/cis_1052.html

Subjects include:
Entry/exit requirements for US citizens
Contact information for the **US Embassy in London** and the **US Consulate in Edinburgh**.
Medical facilities and health information

Medical insurance
The **Smart traveler enrollment program** (STEP)
Traffic safety and road conditions

The Smart Traveler Enrollment Program (STEP) is Interesting
https://travelregistration.state.gov/ibrs/ui/

STEP is a free service provided by the US Government to US citizens who are traveling to a foreign country. By registering information about your upcoming trip abroad with STEP, the US Department of State will be able to assist you better if you experience an emergency while in the UK. It also will be able to help friends and family to get in touch with you in the event of an emergency in the US.

Potterites living in countries other than the US should explore their government's website to obtain similar international travel information and assistance.

The Visit Britain Website
http://www.visitbritain.com/en/US/

Click on **Travel Tips** to reach **Customs and Immigration** information about passports and visas.
http://www.visitbritain.com/en/Travel-tips/Customs-and-immigration/

From that page, click on **Traveller Tips** for links to other important subjects.
http://www.visitbritain.com/en/Travel-tips/Traveller-tips/

Links found on Visit Britain's Traveller Tips directory page include:
Cost of daily items & tipping information
Free guides for your mobile [cell phone]
Medical & health information
Money & currency
Public holidays & time zones
Safety & security
Utilities, weights & measures

Learn About the VAT Tax Before Visiting the UK

When you pay for something in the UK, there often is a **Value Added Tax** (VAT) *included* in the purchase price. The UK VAT is *20%* of the item's commercial value *before* the tax is added—a considerable amount of additional cost.

Business Travelers are the only persons who can recover the UK VAT paid on expenses such as accommodations, car rentals, petrol, and meals.

However, persons traveling to the UK for **pleasure** *can* obtain a full re-fund of the VAT they pay on purchases of goods such as souvenirs, clothing, leather products, and the like—but only when your total purchase at an individual store equals or exceeds £30 ($48), and only if you follow the steps necessary to reclaiming the VAT paid.

The Official British Revenue & Customs VAT Webpage
http://www.hmrc.gov.uk/vat/index.htm

The Official European VAT Webpage
http://www.brvat.com/faq/index.htm

Both of these sites provide extensive information about the UK's VAT system. Unfortunately, much of the information offered is confusing.

Reid Bramblett's *"Getting the VAT Back"* Article

Mr. Bramblett provides a **clear and simple explanation of the UK VAT system**, as well as the best tips for obtaining a VAT refund.
http://www.reidsguides.com/t_mo/t_mo_vat.html

VAT Tip Highlights:

• Every time your total purchase at an individual store equals or exceeds £30, ask the sales clerk for the form needed in order to obtain a VAT refund. Sometimes, the clerk will fill it out for you. Otherwise, be sure that **you** fill out each form at the end of the purchase day—*before* your goodies get distributed throughout your luggage.

• Attach each completed VAT form to its corresponding sales receipt.

• Stash your VAT-attached sales receipts in a single envelope or Zip-bag, so that all your VAT documents are easy to present at the airport's Customs Office when you're ready to go home.

• **When leaving the UK, visit the airport's Customs Office** *before* **you check your luggage!** Although it rarely happens, a Customs Officer may ask to inspect your purchases when examining your sales receipts and VAT forms. If you've already checked the bag(s) containing your purchases, your VAT reclaim forms may be denied.

Peruse the Potterite UK Travel Supplementums

Harry Potter Places **Supplementums** are PDFs freely posted on the Internet, for the benefit of any Potterite planning a UK trip.

Pre-Trip Potter Preparation
http://HarryPotterPlaces.com/tips/PreTripPrep.pdf

Tips for refreshing your Potterverse knowledge before you leave (loading your Pensieve!)—such as enjoying a Potter Film Festival with your friends.

Packing Pointers
http://HarryPotterPlaces.com/tips/PackingPointers.pdf

General UK packing tips, including important methods of baggage identification and travel document copy storage, as well as *vital* personal supplies you'll not want to forget.

Supplies to Purchase *in* the UK
http://HarryPotterPlaces.com/tips/UKtripSupplies.pdf

Stuff you don't need to lug along while traveling to Great Britain, and where to cheaply purchase these items after you arrive.

UK Car Rental and Driving Tips
http://HarryPotterPlaces.com/tips/UKcarRental.pdf

Important considerations for selecting your rental car and preparing to drive in the UK.

UK Telephones
http://HarryPotterPlaces.com/tips/UKphones.pdf

How to dial from outside or inside the UK, and phone options available.

UK Internet Access
http://HarryPotterPlaces.com/tips/UKinternetAccess.pdf

The many options for connecting with the World Wide Web while in the UK, and what services to avoid.

UK Photography Issues
http://HarryPotterPlaces.com/tips/UKphotography.pdf

Railway station photography rules, the value of packing a cheap or disposable camera, and more.

UK Terminology Guide
http://HarryPotterPlaces.com/tips/UKterminology.pdf

A translation of UK English terms that have meanings *different* from the same US English terms.

Lumos Oxford

[©2006 David Iliff]

Best known as home to the oldest and most prestigious English-speaking University in the world, **Oxford** is awesome! The city is cram-packed full of buildings representative of every British architectural style ever conceived and executed. Once the haunt of literary giants such as **JRR Tolkien** and **CS Lewis**, Oxford also abounds with art galleries, museums, churches, colleges, and *shops* of all kinds.
http://www.oxfordcity.co.uk/
http://www.oxfordcityguide.com

Four Iconic Harry Potter Places in Oxford's City Centre

The **Bodleian Library (Site #30)** contains *two* Harry Potter Places:
• **Duke Humfrey's Library** where Hogwarts' Library scenes were shot.

- **The Divinity School** where Hogwarts' Infirmary scenes were filmed, as well as *Goblet of Fire* dance lessons.

👓 Christ Church College (Site #31)

Seen in all eight Harry Potter movies, the **Hogwarts Great Hall** set is an almost-exact reproduction of Christ Church College's **Dining Hall**. Actual location filming for *Sorcerer's Stone* and *Chamber of Secrets* took place on the grand staircase that leads up to the Dining Hall.

👓 New College (Site #32)

Some *Goblet of Fire* courtyard scenes were shot here, including the incident when Mad-Eye Moody turned Draco Malfoy into a white ferret.

A Fifth Harry Potter Film Site is 8 Miles Northwest

👓 Blenheim Palace (Site #29)

Order of the Phoenix flash-back scenes of young Severus Snape being bullied by James Potter and his entourage (Sirius Black, Remus Lupin, and Peter Pettigrew) were shot on the shore of Blenheim Palace's lake, near a readily recognizable tree.

Oxford Parseltongue Pointers:
- Blenheim Palace = "BLEN-um"
- Bodleian = "BOD-lee-an" (*not* "BODE-lee-an")
- Gloucester = "GLAH-ster"
- Oxford = "OX-furd"
- Oxfordshire = "OX-furd-sher"

Planning Your OWLs Visit

Only 50 miles northwest of the UK's capital, Oxford is the most convenient *outside-London* location to visit via public transportation *from* London. Unfortunately, the factors involved in planning an Oxford Potter Places trip are far more complex than those required by any other Potter Place— *especially* if you want to visit **Duke Humfrey's Library.**

In **Specialis Revelio Oxford Part One** we explain the Duke Humfrey's Library access dilemma, and provide in-depth directions for determining the best **manner** and **date** for your OWLs visit.

In **Specialis Revelio Oxford Part Two** we provide several **Suggested Oxford Wizarding Locations Itineraries**. Our itineraries identify the best order for visiting the OWLs on specific days, whether you arrive in Oxford via train, bus, or rental car. Important *time-restrictions* were considered when developing these itineraries, such as the closure of Christ Church College's

Dining Hall (**Hogwarts Great Hall**) from 11:45am to 2:15pm so that students can eat lunch.

In the **Ambulatus Oxford** section you'll find our fantabulous **Oxford Wizarding Locations Map** and directions for walking between Oxford arrival points and the central-city OWLs.

The Oxford Tourist Information Centre
http://www.visitoxfordandoxfordshire.com/

Google Maps UK: 15-16 Broad Street, Oxford OX1 3AS

The **Oxford Tourist Information Centre** (OTIC) office and website are extremely helpful resources for trip planning. OTIC's *Pottering in Harry's Footsteps* tour—the only Oxford-based Harry Potter tour—is discussed in **Specialis Revelio Oxford Part One**.

[©2011 Tara Bellers]

The OTIC's Broad Street shop is also one of the few places in Oxford that offers Harry Potter souvenirs. We suggest you consider including a visit to the OTIC while in Oxford.

Whether or not you'll book a *Pottering* tour, go to the OTIC website after determining your OWL visit date and explore their **Travel & Tourist Info**:

Travel and Transportation Information

This is a great source of information for reaching Oxford via **public transportation**. [Additional train, bus, and driving travel tips are provided in the **Broomsticks to Portkeys** section below.]

Free Oxford Maps and Brochures

The OTIC's **Oxford City Centre Map** identifies non-Potter places in the city.
http://mediafiles.thedms.co.uk/Publication/OS-OX/cms/pdf/Oxford-City-Map2011.pdf

If you're driving to Oxford and want to park *in* the City Centre, download the OTIC's **Oxford Car Park Map**.
http://mediafiles.thedms.co.uk/Publication/OS-OX/cms/pdf/CarParkMap.pdf

Special Offers

The OTIC offers *discounted* **Blenheim Palace and Grounds** tickets online (in advance), or at their Oxford location on the day of your visit—discounts *not* offered by Blenheim Palace in advance or onsite.

Please Note: We suggest you *skip* the OTIC's **Where to Stay** webpage. Refer instead to our upcoming **Lodgings in Oxford** information.

Non-Potter Places in Oxford

The OTIC website offers links to *loads* of non-Potter Oxford places of interest. Because so many Potterites are also Tolkien Fans we offer information about two **JRR Tolkien** Oxford sites.

[©2008 C.D. Miller]

The Eagle & Child Pub
http://en.wikipedia.org/wiki/The_Eagle_and_Child
http://en.wikipedia.org/wiki/Inklings

Google Maps UK: 49 St Giles Street, Oxford OX1 3LU

Operation Hours: Mon-Thurs, 11am to 11pm; Fri-Sat, 10am to 12am; Sundays, 10am to 10:30pm.

Entry Fee: None. Simply purchase a *sip o' something* while visiting.

Visit Time: Schedule at least 45 min here.

Between 1933 and 1949, a few Oxford friends formed an informal writer's group that they called **The Inklings**. **JRR Tolkien** and **CS Lewis** were among the original Inklings. These writers met several times each week to discuss literature and to solicit critiques of passages from their unfinished manuscripts. Inkling luncheon meetings were often held in the **Eagle & Child Pub**, within a private lounge called the **Rabbit Room**.

The Eagle and Child was modernized in 1962, extending the pub through to the building's rear exit, destroying the Rabbit Room's former claim to privacy. Historically interesting commemorative plaques and photos are mounted on the walls of the Inkling's luncheon lounge.

The pub is a 6 minute walk from the Oxford Tourist Information Centre on Broad Street.

🚶 From the OTIC, cross to the opposite side of the street, turn left and walk west on Broad Street. ♦ Turn right at the next street, **Magdalen Street East**, and walk north. At the end of the block is an intersection where Magdalen Street *becomes* **Saint Giles Street**. ♦ Cross to the west side of that intersection and turn right to walk north on Saint Giles Street. ♦ After passing **Pusey Street**, watch on your left for the Eagle & Child pub.

JRR Tolkien's Grave in Wolvercote Cemetery, Oxford
http://en.wikipedia.org/wiki/Wolvercote_Cemetery
http://en.wikipedia.org/wiki/J._R._R._Tolkien

Google Maps UK: Wolvercote Cemetery, OX2 8EE
Address: Wolvercote Cemetery, 447 Banbury Rd, Oxford, Oxfordshire, OX2 8EE

Operation Hours: Mon-Fri, 8am to dusk; Sat, Sun, and Bank Holidays, 9am to dusk.

Entry Fee: None

Visit Time: Schedule at least 45 min here—perhaps an hour.

Parseltongue Pointer:
- Wolvercote = "WOAL-ver-**cot**" (*not* "WOOL-ver-**coat**")

When **John Ronald Reuel Tolkien**'s beloved wife, Edith, died in November of 1971, he had *Lúthien* inscribed beneath her name on the stone that marks her **Wolvercote Cemetery** grave. Twenty-one months later, John Ronald was buried in the same plot, and *Beren* was chiseled beneath his name on their common stone.

Tolkien fans from around the world pilgrimage here. Pens and feathers (representing writing quills) are the most popular tokens placed on the grave.

Even only *casual* Tolkien fans will find themselves profoundly affected by a visit to Tolkien's grave. It cannot be helped. There simply isn't an explanation for the feelings stirred when you kneel beside the final resting place of the mortal man, *Beren*, and *Lúthien* the elf-maiden.

Take a Bus to Wolvercote Cemetery

Go to the Oxford Tourist Information Centre on Broad Street and ask for instructions. They'll explain how to find the nearest bus stop (a block away, on Magdalen Street), and identify which bus you should board to reach the cemetery. The one-way bus trip between Magdalen Street and Wolvercote Cemetery commonly takes 17 minutes. As you disembark, be sure to ask the driver to identify where you should go to catch a bus *back* to Oxford City Centre.

Drive to Wolvercote Cemetery

The one-way drive between **Westgate car park** and Wolvercote Cemetery is approximately 15 minutes. No matter which car park you depart from, use the Wolvercote Cemetery Google Maps UK coordinates to program your SatNav/GPS—or, input the following **cross streets and post code:** Banbury Road and Five Mile Drive, OX2 8EE.

Please Note: Wolvercote Cemetery is *not* located in the **Oxford suburb of Wolvercote.** Don't worry about passing exits or signs to Wolvercote while driving to the cemetery.

Wolvercote Cemetery's main gates are found on **Banbury Road**, just a few feet north of **Five Mile Drive**. If the cemetery gates are open, you can drive in and park by the Chapel. If they are closed, do *not* park on Banbury Road. (The open lane across from the cemetery is a Bus Lane.) Turn around and park on Five Mile Drive.

Once at Wolvercote Cemetery

Inside the cemetery's main gates there is a sign bearing a **map of the graveyard**. Tolkien's grave is in one of the **Roman Catholic** sections—

section **L2**. Additionally, along the paths near the Chapel you'll find small plaques that read "J.R.R. Tolkien, Author," with arrows pointing the way to Tolkien's grave.

[©2008 C.D. Miller]

🚶 With your back to the south side of **Wolvercote Chapel**, take the path that leads south. ♦ Turn right at the next path and walk west until you reach the next path intersection. This is the *southeast corner* of **section L2**. Look ahead and slightly to your right for a **grave surrounded by a low stone enclosure** that will undoubtedly be **packed *full* of plants and flowers**.

Broomsticks to Portkeys: Oxford Transportation Tips

Potterites planning to drive to places outside of London should consider visiting the four central-city OWLs **via Train or Bus** *before* renting a car and leaving London. Driving to Oxford is more convenient only if you'll be squeezing-in a visit to **Blenheim Palace** during the **Five OWLs in One Day** itinerary.

≈ Take a Train to Oxford

Oxford Railway Station [OXF]
http://www.nationalrail.co.uk/

Google Maps UK: Oxford Rail Station, Oxford, Oxfordshire OX1

Trains run between **London's Paddington Railway Station** [PAD] and OXF two or more times *each hour*, from dawn to dark. The one-way journey between PAD and OXF averages 60 minutes.

London/Oxford Return (Round Trip) Adult Fares: £21.50 ($33) during Off-Peak times, £51 ($79) Anytime Travel tickets. Age-related fare discounts are available. Use the **National Rail Journey Planner** to determine Off-Peak ticket times on your day(s) of travel, and to purchase tickets in advance.

✳ OXF has No Luggage Storage or Lockers

If you cannot avoid dragging luggage with you when traveling to Oxford, take an earlier train so that you'll have *at least* 30 extra minutes to stow your bags at one of the two nearby **Backpackers** Hostels.

Oxford Backpackers Hostel
http://www.hostels.co.uk

Google Maps UK: 9A Hythe Bridge Street, Oxford OX1 2EW

Luggage storage £2 ($3.25).

Please Note: The **Oxford Youth Hostel** at 2a Botley Road (a block *west* of OXF) offers luggage storage only to lodgers.

Central Backpackers Hostel
http://www.centralbackpackers.co.uk

Google Maps UK: 13 Park End Street, Oxford OX1 1HH
Luggage storage here is free, which means that storage space fills up quickly.

🚶 Walking directions from OXF to central-city OWLs are provided in the **Ambulatus Oxford** section, and include directions for finding both backpackers hostels.

🚌 Board a Bus to Oxford

Gloucester Green Bus Station [GGBS]
Google Maps UK: Chain Alley, Oxford OX2

Gloucester Green Bus Station & Megabus info:
http://www.tourinaday.com/oxford/bus-station.html

Oxford Tube:
http://www.oxfordtube.com/

Oxford *Espress*:
http://www.oxfordbus.co.uk/

The **Megabus**, **Oxford Tube**, and **Oxford** *Espress* busses leave London's **Victoria Station** every 20 to 30 minutes, sometimes as often as every 10 minutes. Stopping at Marble Arch, Baker Street, Notting Hill Gate, and Shepherd's Bush before heading to Oxford, the fastest one-way bus journey is approximately 1 hour and 40 min during Off-Peak times. No matter what time you leave London, allow at least **2 hours** for your one-way journey *to* Oxford.

    London/Oxford Return (Round Trip) Adult Bus Fare: £16 ($25) if you're returning the same day *or* the next day. Age-related fare discounts are available, and young children accompanying fare-paying adults travel for free. Cheaper fares are available if booked in advance via the Megabus website, but you'll have to commit to specific departure times. If you'll be paying the driver, be sure to have enough **cash** for your fare.

    London/Oxford busses are air-conditioned and equipped with power sockets, free Wi-Fi, and onboard toilets. (Warning: the GGBS has *no* public toilet.)

✳ Gloucester Green Bus Station has No Luggage Lockers

If you cannot avoid dragging luggage with you when traveling to Oxford, take an earlier bus so that you'll have *at least* 30 extra minutes to stow your bags at one of the two **Backpackers** Hostels mentioned in the Oxford Railway Station info above.

🚶 Walking directions from GGBS to central-city OWLs are provided in the **Ambulatus Oxford** section, and include directions for finding both backpackers hostels.

🚌 Bussing to Blenheim

S3 Stagecoach Busses to **Blenheim Palace** leave from OXF or GGBS several times each hour, beginning at 9:15am. A return ticket will cost less than £6 ($9). The Blenheim S3 bus stop is at the **Hensington Gate**, about ½ mile (a 15 min walk) from the Palace and Grounds entrance. Information for using the S3 bus is provided in the **Blenheim Palace (Site #29)** entry.

🚗 Driving to Oxford

✳ **Please Note:** Do *not* plan to drive *into* Oxford City Centre to reach the central-city Oxford Wizarding Locations! Oxford City Centre traffic is extremely heavy every day, all day long, and the one-way street system is incredibly confusing—even for UK natives. Furthermore, finding an open parking space anywhere other than within one of the City Centre car parks is *practically impossible*. Happily, there are five public car parks within a 20- to 30-minute walk of the central-city OWLs.

A **City Centre car parks map** can be found on the Oxford Tourist Information Centre website:
http://mediafiles.thedms.co.uk/Publication/OS-OX/cms/pdf/CarParkMap.pdf

Or at the Oxford.gov website (same map):
http://www.oxford.gov.uk/Direct/78175CarParkMap.pdf

A table demonstrating **City Centre car park fees** can be found at:
http://www.oxford.gov.uk/PageRender/decTS/Car_Park_Charges_occw.htm

A table providing the **nearest Postcode for each City Centre car park** for SatNav/GPS programming can be found at:
http://www.oxford.gov.uk/PageRender/decTS/Car_Parks_occw.htm

The Westgate Shopping Centre Car Park [WCP]
http://www.westgateoxford.co.uk/

Google Maps UK: Westgate Car Park @51.74967,-1.261475

SatNav/GPS: OX1 1NT

Westgate has 1200 parking spaces—more than any other lot inside the city—and offers a multi-storied parking facility (with public toilets), as well as a small surface parking lot. Only a 20 minute walk from the Bodleian ticket office and a 10 minute walk from Christ Church College's visitor entrance, Westgate is the most convenient City Centre car park for Potter purposes.

🚶Walking directions from WCP to central-city OWLs are provided in the **Ambulatus Oxford** section.

All Oxford City Centre Car Parks are open seven days a week from 8am to 8pm. Fees are based on the amount of time you park, and are more expensive on Saturdays. The small surface lots on **Worcester Street** and at **Gloucester Green** cost the most. Below are the *approximate* fees you'll have to pay if parking at **Westgate Car Park** while following our Suggested OWL Itineraries:
- Five OWLs in One Day, Mon-Fri and Sun: £11.50 ($18)
- Five OWLs in One Day, Sat: £14.40 ($22)
- Four OWLs in One Day, Mon-Fri and Sun—if you leave immediately after the last OWL: £17.30 ($27)
- Four OWLs in One Day, Sat—if you leave immediately after the last OWL: £21.70 ($34)

Please Note: To follow a **Five OWLs in One Day** itinerary, you *must* park in a City Centre car park. If you don't mind leaving London about 45 minutes *earlier* than an already-early start, Potterites following a **Four OWLs in One Day** itinerary have the option of using Oxford's **Park & Ride** system.

🚗 🚌 Park for *Free* on the Outskirts of Oxford and Use the Inexpensive Park & Ride System Bus to Reach the City Centre

Operated by the Oxfordshire County Council, all **five** Park & Ride car parks are secure and located along the **Oxford Ring Road**. Parking is free. **Cash-only** Park & Ride Bus tickets for reaching the City Centre can be purchased from the driver.

Return Park & Ride bus fares range from £2.20 to £2.50 ($4) for an individual, with two-person-ticket discounts available. Up to three children under 16 years old can travel free with one fare-paying adult. All Park & Ride buses are wheelchair accessible.

Park & Ride Buses generally leave the car park every 15 minutes. Service begins at 6am on weekdays and Saturdays, with the last bus returning from the City Centre at 11:30pm. On Sundays and Bank Holidays, buses begin running at 8:20am, with the last bus returning from the City Centre at 7pm.

Depending on the time of day and amount of traffic, travel time to the City Centre from **Redbridge** and **Seacourt** car parks is approximately 14 to 17 minutes, 17 to 25 minutes from **Thornhill** car park. **Pear Tree** and **Water Eaton** car parks are north of the city and only used by those arriving from the north.

Several Park & Ride City Centre bus stops are within a 15 min walk from the central-city OWLs. Ask to be let off at the stop closest to the **Bodleian Library** (or another OWL). From there, you can easily find your way around using the **Oxford Wizarding Locations Map** provided in the **Ambulatus Oxford** section.

Please Note: When you disembark, be sure to ask **where to catch the *return bus*.** The return Park & Ride bus stop may be merely across the street. *Or*, it may be a block away.

For Full Oxford Park & Ride System Information Go to:
http://www.oxfordshire.gov.uk

- Scroll down to the **Council services** section
- Click on **Roads and transport**
- Under **Public Transport**, click on **Park and Ride**

In addition to bus fares and time schedules, you'll find each car park's post code (for your SatNav/GPS programming pleasure) under the Park & Ride **Locations** link.

There are **Live Travel Signs** posted along the motorway as you approach Oxford from London, which will warn you if the car park closest to London

is full. If you can access the Internet while enroute to Oxford, use the Park & Ride website's **Live Link** to check space availability at each of the Oxford car parks as you near the city.
http://voyager.oxfordshire.gov.uk/Carpark.aspx

Pottering Around in Oxford

Once you arrive in Oxford's City Centre, all central-city Potter Places lie within short and sweet walking distance of each other. Christ Church College is a 15 minute walk from the other three film sites, which are only a 5 minute walk apart. Thus, you'll need nothing more than your *feet* to travel from one OWL to another.

For Potterites who wish to explore **Non-Potter Places** in Oxford, we provide the following information.

The Oxford Hop-On-Hop-Off Tour Bus
http://www.citysightseeingoxford.com/

Potterites interested in visiting historical non-Potter Oxford places should buy an Oxford Hop-On-Hop-Off (**HOHO**) bus ticket. A 24-hour HOHO ticket costs only £13 ($20) per adult, £10 ($15.50) for Seniors, £11 ($17) for Students, £6 ($9) per 5 to 15 years old child. Family and 48-hour ticket discounts are available on the website.

As with any other HOHO tour bus system, you can hop off the bus at any of the many stops, visit a site, and then return to the bus stop to hop back on the tour bus. Busses generally arrive and leave from each site every 10 to 15 minutes.

If you never hop off, the full Oxford city tour lasts approximately 1 hour.

You can purchase a HOHO ticket from the Oxford Tourist Information Centre, then walk across Broad Street to the nearest HOHO stop and begin your tour, getting off or not getting off, as the spirit moves you.

TAXI Taxis in Oxford

There are Taxis Ranks at OXF and GGBS. Taxis Ranks are also liberally distributed throughout the city. Additionally, Taxis can be hailed from almost any point on any Oxford street. If its **orange light is on**, the Taxi is for hire and you may hail it by simply waving. Minimum taxi fares range from £2.30-2.65 ($4-4.25) to start, plus about £1 per mile.

Potterites who wish to visit **JRR Tolkien's grave** can use a Taxi to reach Wolvercote Cemetery, but it may be difficult to find one to take you *back* to the City Centre.

🛏 Lodgings in Oxford

Throughout all the *Harry Potter Places* travel guidebooks, we do our best to offer tips for finding the types of lodgings you're looking for, based on your budget. Whenever possible, we provide links for finding accommodations that fall within the following three categories:

- **Check in Cheap:** Hostels in or near the City or Village.
- **Board at the Burrow:** City or Village Bed & Breakfast Establishments.
- **Leaky Cauldron to Malfoy Manor:** Livable to Luxurious Hotels in or near the City or Village.

Unfortunately, when it comes to finding safe and sanitary lodgings within **major cities** such as **Oxford**—or London, or Edinburgh—if you're not able to pay big bucks (plenty o' pounds) and stay in a high-priced hotel, it's not easy to accurately assess the quality of accommodation you're looking at online.

Almost all Oxford websites offer accommodation listings, but it's terribly time-consuming to determine which of the listings are actually *in* Oxford.

You can **Google** the type of accommodation you're looking for, such as Oxford, England Hostels … B&Bs … Hotels. But, just like searching for London accommodations, this method is a crapshoot. Any lodging's Internet appearance may be decidedly different from its real-life appearance and quality.

Your Best Bet is to Stay Somewhere Recommended by a Friend

If no one you know has ever stayed in Oxford, your next best bet is to research Oxford lodgings using **Trip Advisor**.
http://www.tripadvisor.com/

When you see an accommodation that seems promising, read the Trip Advisor reviews. If it still seems promising, use **Google** to search for more information about that place.

Specialis Revelio Oxford
Part One

Selecting the Manner and Date of an OWL Visit
'Ware the Ready-Made Harry Potter Oxford Tours

In the **Lumos London** section of *Harry Potter Places* Book One—London and London Side-Along Apparations, we provide information about the most popular Harry Potter Tour companies. Ready-made Harry Potter Tours (**Potted Tours**) are somewhat pricey. But, if you can afford them, they're a marvelous way to accomplish a Potter Place visit without having to personally research and arrange every little detail—*except* **when visiting OXFORD Potter Places!**

Most tour companies offer at least one Potter package that includes travel to Oxford and a guided tour of central-city OWLs. Unfortunately, the vast majority of these tours—even the only **Oxford-based** Harry Potter tour—**do** *not* **include a visit to Duke Humfrey's Library.**

For Potterites who haven't purchased *Harry Potter Places* Book One, we've created a **Potted Tours and Oxford Supplementum**, containing the tours information from **Lumos London**.
http://HarryPotterPlaces.com/b2/PottedToursAndOxford.pdf

Why is Visiting Duke Humfrey's Library Such a Dilemma?
All Tours of Duke Humfrey's Library *Must* be Led by a Guide

Non-Bodleian guides *cannot* take you into Duke Humfrey's Library, under *any* circumstances. If a tour company claims to include Duke Humfrey's Library (**DHL**) in their Oxford Potter package, perhaps they plan to arrange a Bodleian-guided DHL tour for you during the trip they're offering. However, if you book any Potted Oxford tour on a day when university functions are scheduled within DHL, access will be *cancelled* for your visit. Potted Tour companies know this, but may not warn you about it.

All Tours may be *Cancelled* During the First Week of each Term

New Student Orientation functions are frequently scheduled within Duke Humfrey's Library and the Divinity School during first week. We suspect that **term-end** activities also may threaten occasional tour alterations, causing access cancellation to one or both Bodleian Potter Places during the last week of each term.

University Functions May Interfere

University functions may be scheduled in Duke Humfrey's Library or the Divinity School on any day *during* the term.

This doesn't happen often, but when it *does* no Bodleian Tours are allowed entrance to the area being used by the university on that day. University functions are usually scheduled a week or more in advance, and Bodleian Tour staff are the first to be advised when functions will affect their tours.

If a university function *suddenly* has to be held in Duke Humfrey's Library or the Divinity School, advance notice of that area's public-access closure cannot be provided to anyone. Happily, incidents of this kind are rare.

Please Note: *Any* Oxford college or university building can be closed to the public, on *any* day, without *any* advance notice. All the central-city OWLs are actively-operating places of education. Students' needs always have priority over visitors' interests.

Only Two 90-Minute-Long Tours can be Booked in Advance

Tickets for all other Bodleian Tours must be purchased *onsite,* **on the day of the tour**. Onsite Bodleian Tour tickets are offered on a *first-come, first-served* basis as soon as the ticket office opens each day, and they often sellout.

Unless a tour company times your Oxford excursion so that its vehicle rolls into the city at or before the Bodleian ticket office opening time—or sends a representative to secure your Bodleian Tour ticket before your arrival—**no tour company can** *assure* **you** of enjoying Bodleian Library Standard or Mini Tours (tours that include Duke Humfrey's Library).

Only Persons 11 and Older are Allowed to Visit the Library

This is the reason most tour companies cite for not including a Duke Humfrey's Library visit in their Oxford packages.

Staircases and Walking Challenges

There is no lift (elevator) within any of the Old Bodleian buildings. Any Bodleian Tour that includes access to Duke Humfrey's Library requires ascending and descending *twelve,* 5-step staircases, and two individual steps: a grand total of **124 steps**. The 90-minute Bodleian Tours include a few other especially steep staircases, as well as a substantial amount of walking between buildings.

Wheelchair and stair-free access is only available for visiting Old Bodleian ground floor areas: the Divinity School, the Exhibition Room, and the Bodleian Shop.

Self-Guided Divinity-School-Only Tours

Self-Guided tours of the Divinity School are available every day of the week, throughout all opening times, with unlimited tickets available. **Children of all ages are allowed to enjoy the Divinity-School-Only Bodleian Tours.** In fact, children 5 years old and younger can accompany an adult on these tours for free.

[**BTW:** If the Potted Tour company you're considering charges more than £1 per person for a Divinity School visit, they are over-charging you.]

✳ Visiting Duke Humfrey's Library is **not** an option if your party includes children 10 years old or younger—*unless* you have someone willing to take the youngsters on a **Self-Guided Divinity School tour**, while the other adults and older children join a guided Bodleian Tour. If that is a possibility, learn about visiting Oxford independently in the next section.

✳ **If young children or staircases/walking challenges prevent your party from visiting Duke Humfrey's Library, feel free to consider booking** *any* **Ready-Made Harry Potter Oxford Tour.** But, before you actually book a Potted Tour, follow Steps One and Two in the **Determine the Best Date** section below.

We Strongly Recommend an *Independent* OWL Tour

By touring Oxford independently, you'll be free to visit all the central-city OWLs, including Duke Humfrey's Library. You'll also have the option of visiting the *fifth* OWL, **Blenheim Palace.** Potted Tour packages that include travel to Oxford, will not leave enough time to also arrange for a Duke Humfrey's Library visit.

Options for Traveling to Oxford are Abundant

Oxford is the most convenient *outside-London* location to visit via public transportation *from* London. In the Broomsticks to Portkeys section of Lumos Oxford you'll find directions for reaching the city via train or bus (or rental car).

Navigating the Four Central-City OWLs is Easy

Armed with our Oxford Wizarding Locations Map and Walking Directions, it's *easy* to find your way between the four Central-City OWLs. The Oxford Potter maps and walking directions are in the **Ambulatus Oxford** section.

Oxford Wizarding Locations Site Entries

Each of our OWL Site Entries provides basic information about the site and directions to each Potter Pic opportunity found therein. The **Guidebooks** available for purchase at each site will provide all the other information you could possibly wish to know, in addition to being *must-have souvenirs*. Potterites have no need for a Tour Guide!

★**If you feel strongly about having a Tour Guide usher you through Christ Church College and New College**, you may be able to book an **Oxford Tourist Information Centre** tour in *addition* to a Bodleian Duke Humfrey's Library tour. (See Step Three of the next section.)

Determine the Best Date Before Booking *Any* Tour

The more *potential* **Oxford Visit Dates** you can consider, the greater your possibility of accomplishing a Potterly-perfect OWL expedition.

Step One

Avoid scheduling your Harry Potter holiday during Winter Months.

Visiting Oxford between October and Easter can be particularly problematic. Harry Potter Places throughout the UK often have shorter visiting hours, as well as frequent closures, during those months.

New College is only open from 2pm to 4pm each day between October and Easter. Blenheim Palace is only open Wednesdays through Sundays from November to mid-December, and is *closed* from mid-December until February. Christ Church College and the Bodleian are closed during the weeks of Christmas, New Years, and Easter.

School is out for summer during the months of July, August, and September. Those are the best months for scheduling your OWLs visit.

Step Two

Avoid the first and last weeks of the three Oxford University school terms. OWL closures (especially at the Bodleian) are common during these weeks.

Oxford University Term Dates:
- **Michaelmas Term** runs from October through December
- **Hilary Term** begins in January and ends in March
- **Trinity Term** is in session from April to June

If your holiday falls within any term's first or last month, check the specific **term dates** related to your visit by going to the Oxford University website and searching for "dates of term."
http://www.ox.ac.uk

Step Three

Contact Bodleian Library Tour personnel to learn if University Functions are scheduled during your holiday dates. Let them know the dates you may be visiting Oxford and ask which of those days Duke Humfrey's Library and the Divinity School tours are available for touring.

You can Email them: tours@bodleian.ox.ac.uk

Or call them: +44 (0)1865 277224

*If your party includes children 10 years old or younger and you'll be booking an Oxford Potted Tour package, you can **book your Potted Tour** as soon as you discover the date(s) the Divinity School is available, and **skip the remaining steps in this section**.

*If your party consists only of people 11 years old and older, and you're perfectly happy Pottering around Christ Church College and New College on your own (with the help of *Harry Potter Places* and the Guidebooks available at both sites), you can **skip Step Four and jump to Step Five**.

Step Four

If you want a Tour Guide to take you through Christ Church College and New College, check the availability of an Oxford Tourist Information Centre (OTIC) tour. The *Pottering in Harry's Footsteps* tour cannot include Duke Humfrey's Library, but you'll have plenty of time to arrange a Bodleian Tour before or after enjoying the *Pottering* tour.

Go to the OTIC Website
http://www.visitoxfordandoxfordshire.com/

- Put your mouse pointer on the **Our Tours** button, then move your pointer to the **Official Public Tours** button.
- In the drop-down box that appears, click on the **Tours by Type** link.
- Scroll down. Click on the **Pottering in Harry's Footsteps Tour** link.
- Scroll down and click on the new **Pottering in Harry's Footsteps Tour** link.

Once you reach that page, you'll see available OTIC Tour dates.

The OTIC *Pottering in Harry's Footsteps*, this tour is an excellent value! The Adult/Senior/Student fee is only £12 ($19), the Child fee is only £8 ($12). Amazingly, that price includes *all* entrance fees—at least a £10 ($15) value for adults. Plus, the OTIC Tour Guide can whisk you past any **entrance queue** and take you directly into the site.

Unfortunately, OTIC *Pottering* tours are not often offered. None are ever scheduled in December or January. In November, the *Pottering* tour is only offered on **one Saturday**. During each of the other months, the *Pottering* tour is only offered on **one Friday**—except for July and August, when it is offered on **two Fridays** each month.

Please Note: Due to the *Pottering in Harry's Footsteps* tour's infrequent availability, and the fact that it *can* **be booked in advance**, OTIC *Pottering* tours often sell-out.

If a *Pottering* tour isn't available on one of your potential OWL dates, consider booking a **Private Oxford Tourist Information Centre tour**.

No, a private OTIC tour cannot include entrance to Duke Humfrey's Library.

Yes, a private OTIC tour is quite expensive when compared to the *Pottering* tour fee. But, if you'll be traveling with three or more companions, the private tour base fee (£89/$138) becomes more reasonable: only £22.25 ($35) each for a party of four, for example. Up to 19 people can split the OTIC private tour base fee.

Please Note: Entrance fees are *not* included in the OTIC private tour base fee. Be prepared to pay another £10 ($15) per adult, in order to visit the OWLs.

Private OTIC tours are available in the mornings or afternoons on almost any day of the year, and foreign language guides may be available. Your private Tour Guide can meet you at the Oxford train station, or anywhere else in the City Centre—even at your City Centre lodgings.

Download the **OTIC Booking Pack** to learn all about private tour base fees, extra charges, and other tour information. The Booking Pack also includes the private tour booking form.
http://mediafiles.thedms.co.uk/Publication/OS-OX/cms/pdf/W-T_booking_pack2011.pdf

★If your party includes children 10 years old or younger, you can **book your *Pottering* Tour now**, **skipping all remaining Steps**.

★If your party consists only of people 11 years old and older, **do not book an OTIC tour** until you've accomplished Step Five.

Step Five

Decide which Bodleian Tour you want to take. If you're interested in the OTIC *Pottering* tour, and it's available during your visit, reserve a **1:45pm to 3:45pm** time slot for the *Pottering* tour on your independent OWLs itinerary before considering which Bodleian Tour to take.

The Bodleian Library offers **four** tours that include access to both of the Harry Potter film sites, and **two** tours that do *not* include Duke Humfrey's Library. Each Bodleian Tour has a separate webpage providing in-depth (and most up-to-date) information that can be accessed from the Bodleian Tours directory.
http://www.bodleian.ox.ac.uk/bodley/about/visitors/individual

To help you quickly *compare* the Bodleian Tours, we prepared a table demonstrating the most Potterly-important points of each. You can find the *Harry Potter Places* **Bodleian Library Tours Supplementum** at:
http://HarryPotterPlaces.com/b2/BodleianToursSupplementum.pdf

If your potential OWL visit dates coincide with one of the 90-minute Bodleian Tours, consider spending a little extra to **prebook** a tour that includes the Divinity School *and* Duke Humfrey's Library. If you don't want to continue on the 90-minute tour after enjoying the Bodleian Potter Places, you can always politely excuse yourself and leave.

Please Note: Be sure not to simply *disappear* from the tour! Beyond being rude, that action might trigger an unnecessary **Search and Rescue operation**.

To Prebook One of the Bodleian's Two 90-Minute Tours

Extended tours cannot be booked earlier than a week in advance, but you can be put on a waiting list for the tour up to four months ahead of time.

Begin by Emailing Bodleian Tour personnel: tours@bodleian.ox.ac.uk

Do not send any financial information. Simply identify that you're interested in prebooking one of the 90-minute tours, and ask for their assistance in selecting the best possible tour from the dates you're able to spend in Oxford.

If Bodleian personnel identify a 90-minute tour and date that can reasonably assure you of being able to visit *both* Bodleian Potter places, **prebook that tour** and schedule the rest of your OWLs around it.

If You'll *NOT* be Prebooking a 90-Minute Bodleian Tour

Plan your OWLs visit around an early morning arrival in Oxford, so that you can reach the Bodleian Wooden Lodge ticket office when it opens and purchase a first-come, first-served **Bodleian Standard** or **Mini Tour** ticket for later in the day.

The Bodleian ticket office opens at **9am Mon-Fri, 9:15am Sat, 11am Sun.**

Please Note: The Bodleian ticket office only accepts **cash**.

Step Six

You've determined your best OWL visit date and selected a Bodleian Tour.

If you haven't already, prebook everything that you possibly can NOW!

Pre-Trip Transport Times Check

Two weeks before your holiday, check the transport times of your selected itinerary. Any number of events may have altered the bus or train times we investigated to create the *Harry Potter Places* Suggested OWLs Itineraries. If associated transport schedules have changed, site visiting times within each itinerary may need to be adjusted.

PART TWO

Suggestions for Visiting the Oxford Wizarding Locations

The *Harry Potter Places* **Suggested OWL Itineraries** provided at the end of this section are designed for Potterites who wish to **independently** visit Oxford Wizarding Locations in as rapid and efficient manner as Potterly possible, and who will *not* be:

- Booking any Ready-Made Harry Potter tour.
- Prebooking a 90-minute Bodleian Library tour.

Happily, Potterites who **will** be prebooking a 90-minute Bodleian Library tour can use our individual **OWL Site Entries** and the Suggested OWL Itineraries to develop your own method of visiting the OWLs.

To further assist you, we've prepared tables demonstrating the Standard Open Times for all five OWLs, as well as their winter closure times. You can find the **OWLs Open Times Supplementum** at:
http://HarryPotterPlaces.com/b2/OWLsOpenTimes.pdf

What a Difference a Date Makes

All of our Suggested OWL Itineraries are based on visiting Oxford **between Easter and mid-October**. If you visit Oxford during winter months, you'll likely need to alter the itinerary you follow. A **Five OWLs in One Day itinerary is *not possible*,** for example, **between mid-October and Easter** because New College is only open from 2pm to 4pm.

The Best Way to Visit All Five OWLs

You really should schedule **two days in Oxford** to visit all Five OWLs, so that you can fully enjoy the **Blenheim Palace** experience by touring its *interior* as well as trekking to its little lakeside OWL.

You'll not necessarily have to pay for overnight Oxford lodging to do a two-day trip. You can stay in London and inexpensively travel via bus or train to Oxford on both days. But, please keep in mind that many Oxford lodging options are less expensive than those in London. Staying overnight in Oxford might be a good thing.

The **Oxford Tourist Information Centre** offers *discounted* **Blenheim Palace, Park & Gardens** tickets both online (prebooked) and onsite at the Broad Street OTIC location. The OTIC Palace, Park & Gardens adult tickets cost £16 ($25). That's only £5 ($8) more than a ticket for only the Park & Gardens.

Similarly discounted senior/student/child Palace, Park & Gardens tickets are also available at the OTIC. [Blenheim Palace does not offer discounted tickets of any kind online.]

Additionally, allowing two days to visit Oxford will afford you the ability to enjoy many non-Potter Oxford places. You can tour the city via the **Oxford Hop-On-Hop-Off Bus**. You can visit **JRR Tolkien** and **CS Lewis** Oxford sites. You can enjoy several of the many art galleries, museums, churches, and *shops* found in Oxford.

We highly recommend that Potterites review the **Blenheim Palace (Site #29)** entry, and consider spending **two days** in Oxford before selecting a Five OWLs in One Day itinerary.

The Downside of Visiting Five OWLS in One Day

Visiting the **Blenheim Palace Park** during a one-day trip to Oxford is *doable*— but only allows for a very short fifth OWL visit. Granted, the Blenheim OWL is naught but a tree on the bank of a lake and doesn't require a lengthy visit. But a ton of time and expense is required to squeeze-in a trip to Blenheim during your one day in Oxford, merely to snap a few lakeside-tree-pix.

Five OWLs in One Day Time and Expense Considerations

A **Blenheim Park & Gardens** ticket (no Palace entry) costs £11 ($17), whether you purchase it in advance from the Blenheim website or at the Blenheim gate. The OTIC does not offer discounted Park & Gardens tickets.

The Oxford/Blenheim Return trip **Stagecoach S3 Bus** fare is only £6 ($10), but taking the bus can cost you up to *90 minutes* of travel time during your one day in Oxford.

If driving to Blenheim (*60 minutes* of travel time during your one day in Oxford), in addition to your petrol expense and the Park & Gardens ticket fee, you *must* park in a **City Centre car park**. There simply isn't enough time to use the **Oxford Park & Ride system**, so that you can park for **free** and catch a **cheap bus** into the City Centre. When driving to a Five OWLs in One Day itinerary, the *minimum* City Centre car park fees will range from £11.50 ($19) on Sundays through Fridays, to £14.40 ($24) on Saturdays.

Five OWLs in One Day Blenheim Visit Time Limits

Whether you drive or bus here, you'll **not** have enough time to also visit the *interior* of Blenheim Palace. On Mondays through Saturdays, you'll have plenty of time to visit the fifth OWL and the Blenheim exterior Flagstaff Gift shop and Ice Cream Parlour (café). On Sundays, your Blenheim OWL and shop visit will be short, and visiting on a Sunday will cost you *10 minutes* at Christ Church College—a much more important OWL!

Five OWLs in One Day Additional Stress Factors

 Walking Woes

Even if you'll be driving to Oxford and Blenheim, accomplishing a Five OWLs in One Day itinerary may be *too much walking* for young children, seniors, and portly Potterites. If you'll be bussing to Blenheim, in addition to all the between-central-city-OWLs walking, at least **two *sprint*-like walks** are required to stay on schedule.

Bus Bothers

The Oxford/Blenheim S3 Schedule may change. Bus times found within all our OWL itineraries are based on the November, 2010, **Stagecoach S3 bus schedule**. [**Please Note:** This schedule was still considered current in December of 2011.]
http://www.stagecoachbus.com/PdfUploads/Timetable_8898_S3.pdf

If you'll be bussing to Blenheim while following a Five OWLs in One Day itinerary, *be very sure* to double-check the Stagecoach S3 bus schedule during your Pre-Trip Transport Times Check. Missing any itinerary-indicated bus between Oxford and Blenheim may cause you to miss the Blenheim OWL, or miss your train/bus back to London.

Additionally, all Bus schedules are based on a best-case-traffic scenario. Any number of factors might cause unforeseen bus schedule delays or alterations on any day.

Driving Dilemmas

Even when using a SatNav/GPS device, it is possible to accidentally take a wrong turn, increasing the time required to drive between Oxford and Blenheim. Congested traffic conditions will increase the drive time. Accidents or unscheduled road closures may require you to alter the route to Blenheim, increasing your drive time and prompting ugly arguments with your SatNav/GPS device.

Again, if you take two days to visit Oxford you'll be able to enjoy full-length visits at all Five OWLs—and lots more!

The *Harry Potter Places* Suggested OWL Itineraries

Each Suggested OWL Itinerary Identifies:

• The most efficient order for visiting Oxford Wizarding Locations on specific days. [*Time-dependent* visit restrictions were considered, such as the closure of Christ Church College's Dining Hall (**Hogwarts Great Hall**) from **11:45am to 2:15pm** so that students can eat lunch.]

• The maximum amount of time for between-OWL travel, as well as on-site time.

🚶 Walking Directions

Directions for traveling between the four central-city OWLs—as well as for traveling between the train station, bus station, car parks and the OWLs—are in the **Ambulatus Oxford** section. Oxford City Centre walking directions are *not* provided within the Suggested Itineraries. Blenheim Palace walking directions are found within its site entry.

We Strongly Suggest that You Pack a Lunch

You'll have ample time to buy *snacks* at various OWLs while following our itineraries, but not enough time to catch a real meal, *anywhere*—especially if following a Five OWL in One Day itinerary. See the **Supplies to Purchase in the UK** *Harry Potter Places* Supplementum for packed lunch tips.
http://HarryPotterPlaces.com/tips/UKtripSupplies.pdf

OWL Itineraries ICON Key

🚌 **GGBS** = Gloucester Green Bus Station

🚆 **OXF** = Oxford Railway Station

🚗 **WCP** = Westgate Car Park. Other **Oxford City Centre car parks** may be used, but we only provide travel times from this lot.

🚻 = A Public Toilet. There are *no public toilets* in the Bodleian Library complex. Our itineraries identify when and where you'll encounter them elsewhere.

A bold "at" symbol [@] indicates that you must pay strict attention to the time. To keep on schedule, arrive at, or leave from, a site *no later* than the time specified.

The *Harry Potter Places* **Oxford Wizarding Locations Map** that identifies each OWL's location is included with each itinerary. It also is available separately, in the **Ambulatus Oxford** section.

Harry Potter Places Suggested Itineraries

All Five OWLs in One Day

On Mondays through Saturdays
http://HarryPotterPlaces.com/b2/208aAllFiveMtoSat.pdf

🚆🚌 On Sundays: Traveling via Train or Bus to Oxford
http://HarryPotterPlaces.com/b2/208bAllFiveSunPublicTrans.pdf

🚗 On Sundays: Driving to Oxford
http://HarryPotterPlaces.com/b2/208cAllFiveSunCar.pdf

Four Central-City OWLs in One Day

On Mondays through Saturdays
http://HarryPotterPlaces.com/b2/208dFourMtoSat.pdf

On Sundays
http://HarryPotterPlaces.com/b2/208eFourSunday.pdf

Potterites enjoying two days in Oxford can visit all of Blenheim Palace—and enjoy many other Oxford sites—on the day before or after following a **Four Central-City OWLs in One Day** itinerary.

AMBULATUS OXFORD

Potterite's Guide to Ambulating (Walking) Around Oxford

The Oxford Wizarding Locations Map

We created the **Oxford Wizarding Locations (OWLs) Map** using map images obtained from **Google Maps UK**. The *Harry Potter Places* OWLs Map identifies the best routes to follow when walking between central-city OWLs.

[Underlying Map Images © 2011 Google]
http://HarryPotterPlaces.com/b2/OWLsMap.pdf

The *Harry Potter Places* **Suggested OWL Itineraries**—found in **Specialis Revelio Oxford Part Two**—each contain the OWLs Map (and its key), and identify the best order for visiting the OWLs on specific days. The OWLs Map link above is provided for Potterites who plan to design a personal Oxford itinerary. Happily, **all** Potterites can use the directions below to follow *Harry Potter Places* itineraries, *or* to ambulate around Oxford in your own way.

Walking from Oxford Points of Arrival to the OWLs

To keep the OWLs Map as clear (large print) and easy to follow as possible, we limited it to the central-city OWLs area. Oxford's Railway Station, the Gloucester Green Bus Station, and the Westgate Car Park *do not appear* on the map.

Individual **Oxford-Arrival-Point-to-OWL** walking directions, with close-up, large print map segments, are posted online as *Harry Potter Places* **Supplementums**. Once you've determined your mode of transportation to Oxford, download the appropriate Directions Supplementum.

Each of Our Directions Supplementums will Guide You to:
- The **Bodleian Library Great Gate** and ticket office.
- **Christ Church College**—in case you've prebooked a 90-minute Bodleian tour, or will *not* be visiting Duke Humfrey's Library.
- **New College**—another OWL tour start-option if you don't need to purchase a Bodleian tour ticket.

Directions Supplementums

⇄ Oxford Railway Station to OWLs
http://HarryPotterPlaces.com/b2/OXFtoOWLs.pdf

⊟ Gloucester Green Bus Station to OWLs
http://HarryPotterPlaces.com/b2/BusToOWLs.pdf

⊟ OWLs to Blenheim Bus
http://HarryPotterPlaces.com/b2/OWLsToBus.pdf

Potterites bussing to Blenheim Palace during a Five OWLs in One Day itinerary can easily find their way back to the Gloucester Green Bus Station. (If you arrived Oxford by train, you passed the GGBS enroute to the Bodleian Library.) However, we developed this Supplementum for Potterites who want specific directions and maps for reaching the GGBS from each of the OWLs.

Please Note: This Supplementum also includes directions for walking from the GGBS to the Oxford Railway Station.

🚕 Westgate Car Park to OWLs
http://HarryPotterPlaces.com/b2/WCPtoOWLs.pdf

🚕⊟ Driving Potterites Using the Oxford Park & Ride System

The **Oxford Wizarding Locations Map** will help you navigate from any Centre City Park & Ride bus stop to the central-city OWLs.

Map with the Centre City Owls *and* Oxford Arrival Points

Download the **Oxford City Map** from the Oxford Tourist Information Centre's website.
http://mediafiles.thedms.co.uk/Publication/OS-OX/cms/pdf/Oxford-City-Map2011.pdf

Walking Between the Central-City OWLs Using Our Map

Alternative Routes

The **solid red lines** seen on the OWLs Map indicate the primary between-OWL routes we describe below. However, you'll notice some **dotted red line** routes on the OWLs Map. These are **alternative routes** between OWLs. You can easily follow these alternative routes if—for instance—you want to visit the Market Street public toilets, or if you miss the pedestrian lane that leads from High Street to Radcliffe Square.

The dotted red line route between Point A and the **Point D** on **Holywell Street** is the Mid-October to Easter route to New College from the Bodleian Library described below.

Bodleian Library to the Christ Church College Visitor Entrance
Point A to Point B on the Oxford Wizarding Locations Map
A 15 minute walk.

🚶 Exit the **Bodleian Library** via the **Great Gate** on **Catte Street**. ♦ Turn right and walk south on Catte Street, watching on your left for **Radcliffe Square**. ♦ Turn left and follow Radcliffe Square to the west, and then south, to walk around the **Radcliffe Camera** building. ♦ Once on the west side of the Radcliffe Camera, continue south along the *pedestrian lane* that leads between two buildings, until you reach **High Street**. ♦ Turn right at High Street and walk west to **Saint Aldate's** (street). ♦ Turn left and walk south on the east side of Saint Aldate's. Walk *past* the Christ Church building with its prominent **Tom Tower**, watching on your left for **the elaborate iron gate that leads to Christ Church Meadow.** ♦ **Turn left and go through the gate. Follow the wide stone path east, watching on your left for the Christ Church College Visitor Entrance.**

Bodleian Library to Christ Church College Canterbury Entrance

Point A to Point C on the Oxford Wizarding Locations Map
A 10 minute walk.

🚶 Exit the **Bodleian Library** via the **Great Gate** on **Catte Street**. ♦ Turn right and walk south to **High Street**. Look to your right for the crosswalk that leads to the south side of High Street. ♦ Turn right and walk west on the south side of High Street, watching on your left for a *pedestrian lane* called

41

Oriel Street. ♦ Turn left to walk south on Oriel Street until you reach **Oriel Square** (street). Continue south to the end of Oriel Square. The **Christ Church College Canterbury Gate** will be on your right.

Christ Church College Visitor Entrance to the Bodleian Library
Point B to Point A on the Oxford Wizarding Locations Map
A 15 minute walk.

🚶 Exit from the **Christ Church College Visitor Entrance**. ♦ Turn right and walk east on the stone path that leads to **Saint Aldate's** (street). ♦ Turn right and walk north until you cross to the north side of **High Street**. ♦ Turn right and walk east, watching on your left for a *pedestrian lane* leading north. The first place you'll reach that looks like a pedestrian lane *isn't* one—it's an *alley* that eventually becomes **Turl Street**. The *next* opening that looks like a pedestrian lane *is* one. ♦ Turn left and walk north, reaching the west **Radcliffe Square** walkway. Continue north past the **Radcliffe Camera** building, following the walkway when it curves east, until you reach **Catte Street**. ♦ Turn left and walk north, watching on your left for the **Bodleian Library Great Gate**.

Christ Church College Canterbury Gate to the Bodleian Library
Point C to Point A on the Oxford Wizarding Locations Map

A 10 minute walk.

The **Christ Church College Canterbury Gate** exit that leads to **Merton Street/Oriel Square** is closer to the other central-city OWLs than the Christ Church College Visitor Entrance/Exit, and is easy to find.

The *Christ Church Guide to College and Cathedral* brochure you'll receive when entering (from any gate or entrance) contains an excellent map of the college's interior. Locate the **Picture Gallery**. There you'll see the Canterbury Gate exit.

🚶 Exit **Christ Church College** from the **Canterbury Gate**. ♦ Turn left to walk north on **Oriel Square** (street). ♦ At the point where the street curves left and becomes **King Edward Street**, keep *right* to continue north on a *pedestrian lane* called **Oriel Street**, until you reach **High Street**. ♦ Directly across High Street is the pedestrian lane that leads to the **Radcliffe Square** walkway. Because it may be *unsafe* for you to cross here, we suggest that you don't. ♦ Turn right and walk east on the south side of High Street to the next crosswalk. ♦ Turn left and cross to the north side of High Street, then look to your right (east) for the **Catte Street** *pedestrian lane*. ♦ Walk north up that lane. After passing the **Radcliffe Camera** building, watch on your left for the **Bodleian Library Great Gate**.

Directions from Christ Church College to New College
Points B or C to Point D on the Oxford Wizarding Locations Map
A 15 to 25 minute walk.

🚶 Follow the directions above from either Point B (**Christ Church College Visitor Entrance**) or Point C (**Christ Church College Canterbury Gate**) to Point A (the **Bodleian Library Great Gate**). Then follow the directions below from Point A to Point D (**New College**).

Directions from the Bodleian Library to New College

Point A to Point(s) D on the Oxford Wizarding Locations Map

[©2011 Tara Bellers]

Easter to Mid-October

A 5 minute walk.

🚶 Exit the **Bodleian Library** via the **Great Gate** on **Catte Street**. ◆ Turn left and walk north on Catte Street. ◆ Turn right at the next street, **New College Lane**. You'll see a marvelous arched bridge connecting the buildings on either side of the lane: the **Hertford College bridge**, aka the *Bridge of Sighs*. ◆ Walk east, passing under the arched bridge. ◆ Continue following New College Lane as it turns south, and then east again, until you reach the entrance to **New College**.

Mid-October to Easter
A 10 minute walk.

🚶 Exit the **Bodleian Library** via the **Great Gate** on **Catte Street**. ♦ Turn left and walk north, *past* **New College Lane**, to the intersection of Catte Street with **Broad Street** (on the left) and **Holywell Street** (on the right). ♦ Turn right and walk east on Holywell Street. ♦ After passing **Mansfield Road**, watch on your right for a **driveway** that leads beneath **an arched stone opening**. ♦ Turn right and walk inside, looking for a **New College Porter**. If you reach the **Holywell Quadrangle** (a large grassy area) without finding a Porter, turn right and look right for the **New College Porter's Lodge**.

Directions from New College to Christ Church College
Point(s) D to Point B on the Oxford Wizarding Locations Map
A 15 to 25 minute walk.

Reverse the directions above, between the two New College entrances and the **Bodleian Library's Great Gate**. From there, follow the **Point A** to **Point B** directions found above to walk from the Bodleian Library to Christ Church College.

29

BLENHEIM PALACE

Young Severus Snape's Lakeside Study Tree
http://www.blenheimpalace.com/
http://en.wikipedia.org/wiki/Blenheim_Palace

Google Maps UK: Woodstock, Oxfordshire OX20 1PX, UK

Blenheim Palace Travel information: See below.

Operation Hours and Entry Fees: See below.

Visit Time: Enjoying everything offered by Blenheim Palace and Gardens could easily fill an entire day.

At the very least, schedule 3 hours on site to enjoy a guided State Room tour of the palace and the Churchill Exhibition, in addition to visiting the Blenheim OWL and Palace shops.

Add another hour to tour one or two of the award-winning Blenheim Gardens.

Add yet another hour to visit the Blenheim Stable's Indoor Cinema and watch documentaries related to Palace history and the many movies filmed here.

The **Five OWLs in One Day** itineraries (see **Specialis Revelio Oxford**) allow for only a *very brief* Blenheim OWL and exterior shop visit.

Parseltongue Pointers:
- Blenheim Palace = "BLEN-um"
- Marlborough = "MALL-burra"

[©2004 Gailf548]

Blenheim Palace is the only non-royal country house in England to hold the title of Palace. One of the largest houses in England, construction began in 1705, but a plethora of political problems delayed its completion until 1724. The United Nations Educational, Scientific and Cultural Organization (UNESCO) recognized Blenheim Palace as a **World Heritage Site** in 1987.

The Palace originated as a gift from Queen Anne, the first sovereign of the Kingdom of Great Britain, to John Churchill, the first Duke of Marlborough, in honor of his victory over the French at the battle of Blenheim in 1704. (The fact that John was married to Sarah Jennings, Anne's closest friend and confidant, surely had *nothing* to do with her gift.) In return, the Duke and Duchess ensured that their home became a monument to Queen Anne, despite the fact that she failed to finance the entirety of its construction.

Blenheim Palace also happens to be famous as the birthplace of **Sir Winston Churchill**, Prime Minister of Britain during WWII.

Designed in the rare English Baroque style of architecture, Blenheim Palace is also unique in its combined usage as a family home, mausoleum, and national monument. Several different styles of gorgeous formal pleasure gardens can be found here, and the Palace is surrounded by 2000 acres of lovely parkland.

The Churchill family has spent over 300 years adding to Blenheim's colossal collection of paintings, porcelain, furniture, statues, and tapestries. Each Churchill generation has worked tirelessly to ensure the preservation of this national treasure, often at great personal expense.

The Blenheim OWL is Naught but a Lakeside Tree

During the last occlumency lesson inflicted upon him by Professor Snape in *Order of the Phoenix*, Harry accidentally invaded Snape's mind. There, he experienced the memory of young Severus being bullied by James Potter and his entourage (Sirius Black, Remus Lupin, and Peter Pettigrew). These flash-back scenes were shot on the shore of Blenheim Palace's lake, in the vicinity of a readily recognizable tree.

Site Rating

Blenheim Palace is Assigned a Might-be-Fun Rating:

• When following a **Five OWLs in One Day** itinerary, it will take up to **4 hours** to reach this site, snap your tree pix, and return to Oxford — *without* allowing time to visit the Palace interior or its Pleasure Gardens.

• Admission to only the Park and Gardens (OWL admission) costs £11.50 ($18) for adults.

• The screenshot reproduction pix available here involve little more than a tree with a big hole in it.

Many Potterites consider this time and cash expenditure excessive in relationship to what little can be photographed. However, Potterites who enjoy touring historic buildings and gardens will be thrilled by all that Blenheim Palace has to offer.

Blenheim Palace Opening Times

The 2000-acre Park surrounding Blenheim Palace (including the OWL site) is open year-round from 9am to 6pm or dusk, closed only on Christmas day.

From the second week of February to the last week of October, Blenheim Palace and Gardens are open seven days a week, from 10:30am to 5:30pm.
• The exterior Flagstaff Gift Shop is open from 10am to 5:30pm.
• The exterior Ice Cream Parlour (café) is open from 11am to 4pm.
• The Churchill Shop is open from 11am to 5pm.
• The Palace Shop is open from 11am to 5:30pm.
• The Pantry café, Water Terrace café, and Indian Room restaurant are open from 10am to 5:30pm.
• The Pleasure Gardens Café and Shop are open from 10:30am to 5pm.
• All Palace, Garden, and Park areas must be vacated by 6pm.

From November to mid-December, Blenheim Palace and Gardens are open only on Wednesdays through Sundays, at the hours seen above.
    The Blenheim Palace and Gardens are *closed* from mid-December to the second week of February.

Blenheim Palace Admission Options

A **Palace, Park & Gardens ticket** includes admission to:
• Blenheim Palace interior, all of its shops, cafés, and restaurants.
• The Churchill Exhibition.
• Guided tours of the State Rooms.
• The Untold Story exhibit rooms.
• *All* of the Blenheim Gardens, external exhibits, and Park (below).

A **Park & Gardens ticket** includes admission to:
- The Formal Gardens, which include the Secret Garden, Rose Garden, Temple of Diana, the Arboretum, and Cascade.
- The Pleasure Gardens, which include the Marlborough Maze, an Adventure Play Area, the Butterfly House, the Lavender Garden, and the Blenheim Bygones exhibit.
- The Miniature Train ride to the Pleasure Gardens.
- The Stables, where you'll find the Churchill's Destiny exhibition and the Indoor Cinema.
- Several of the shops and cafés.

Blenheim Palace Buggies

When the weather is pleasant you can enjoy a 20 minute tour of the Lake and Park while riding in a 7-seat motorized buggy. Tickets are available at the Flagstaff Kiosk next to the main palace entrance and cost £3.50 ($6) for adults, £2.50 ($4) for seniors, students, or children. Although it's not horse-drawn, you're sure to enjoy this personally-guided tour of the grounds.

Blenheim Palace Special Events

Check the Blenheim Palace website to learn of Special Events being held during your visit, such as jousting, musical performances, and outdoor theatre. Some of these events are free!

Blenheim Palace Admission Fees

Palace, Park & Gardens Tickets
Purchased on the Blenheim Palace website or at a Blenheim Gate:
Adults £20 ($31); Seniors or Students £15.50 ($24); Children 5-16 y/o £11 ($17); under 5s are free.

Discounted Palace, Park & Gardens Tickets
Purchased on the Oxford Tourist Information Centre website or at the OTIC Broad Street office in Oxford:

Adults £16.50 ($26); Seniors or Students £14 ($22); Children 5-16 y/o £9.50 ($15); under 5s are free. [Discounted Park & Gardens tickets are not available from Blenheim Palace.]

Park & Gardens Tickets
Purchased on the Blenheim Palace website or at a Blenheim Gate:

Adults £11.50 ($18); Seniors or Students £8.50 ($13); Children 5-16 y/o £6 ($9); under 5s are free. [Discounted Park & Gardens tickets are not available from the OTIC.]

Park-Only Tickets

On days during the winter, when the Palace and Gardens are closed, a small Park admission is charged at the gate: Adults, £4.50 ($7), Seniors/Students/Children £3.50 ($6).

Ambulatus Blenheim

Whether you drive or bus to Blenheim, you'll eventually arrive at a large gravel yard in front of the Main Palace entrance. Look to your right. At the Palace's northeastern corner is a sidewalk that leads to the exterior Flagstaff Gift Shop and Ice Cream Parlour. (Public toilets are located here, as well.)

Just *before* the northeastern corner sidewalk is a path that leads north, and then curves west, heading toward the **Grand Bridge** that separates **Blenheim Lake** from the **Queen Pool**. To reach the Blenheim OWL, follow this path until you can turn right and walk across the Grand Bridge.

[©2008 C.D. Miller]

Severus' tree has such a huge hole in it, you'll recognize where *Order of the Phoenix* flash-back scenes were shot even before you reach the Grand Bridge. In fact, you'll be snapping your first Potter Pic while walking *over* the bridge.

49

Blenheim Potter Pic #1

[*Order of the Phoenix* screenshot segment (enhanced)]

This screenshot cannot be perfectly recreated unless you're in a boat on the lake. Happily, Potterites can snap a similar shot while walking over the Grand Bridge.

[©2008 C.D. Miller]

If you wisely decided to dedicate two days for visiting Oxford and have time to enjoy all that Blenheim Palace has to offer, you'll have plenty of time to send one or more of the others in your party to sit in young Severus' place beside the tree before you snap.

Upon reaching the north side of the Grand Bridge you'll find a sad sign.

[©2008 C.D. Miller]

However, just beyond it is a **wooden gate** that guards what could reasonably be *considered* a **footpath**, leading toward the Snape Tree area. As you can see in the pic above right, there was **no fence** on either side of this gate in October of 2008.

Blenheim Park fences are wire-mesh-and-metal-stake units that can be *moved* from place to place, and attached to any of the wooden gates found in several areas around the grounds. These mobile fence units are specially designed to enclose the Blenheim **sheep** within one Park area at a time, so that they can "mow" the grass there.

[©2008 C.D. Miller]

In October of 2008, a fence unit was in place to enclose the **Column of Victory** monument grounds. A flock of Blenheim sheep can barely be seen happily munching and mowing — way in the distance!

Please Note: We are *not* advising Potterites to **violate** the Blenheim "keep to roads and footpaths" sign. And we hereby disclaim responsibility for any liability or penalty, resulting directly or indirectly from any person or persons who independently elect to do so after reading this travel guidebook.

We are merely reporting that: In October of 2008, when CD Miller found the unfenced gate just beyond the sign at the north end of the Grand Bridge, she walked around it and followed the dirt path behind it toward the area of Severus' tree. After *leaving the dirt path*, she quickly reached Severus' tree and quietly snapped several Potter Pix in the tree's vicinity. Blenheim security personnel did not appear while she was doing so, nor did they accost her after she returned to the paved path.

Thus, it stands to reason that similarly quick and quiet Potterites could probably make your way to the area of Severus' tree and snap the following Blenheim Potter Pix without encountering any difficulties or reprimands.

Bottom Line, Please Remember the Potterite Prime Directive:

To *POLITELY* Go Where Potterites Need to Go
– without **PERTURBING** anybody –
So That Other Potterites Can *Continue*
to ENJOY GOING THERE.

Blenheim Potter Pic #2

[*Order of the Phoenix* screenshot (enhanced)]

It's such a shame that there's nothing similar to Hogwarts Castle seen to the west of this tree in real-life. However, Potterites with Photoshop talents can insert an image similar to that seen in the screenshot.

Blenheim Potter Pix #3 & #4

These last two scenes were shot in the grassy area found behind (north of) Severus' tree.

[*Order of the Phoenix* screenshots (enhanced) above and below]

After snapping your Blenheim OWL Potter Pix, return to the Grand Bridge and walk back toward the palace to reach the Flagstaff Gift Shop and Ice Cream Parlour. In 2008, there were no Harry Potter souvenirs available. If that hasn't changed, you still can purchase Blenheim Palace souvenirs there.

If you have a **Palace, Park and Gardens** ticket, ask Flagstaff Gift Shop or Café personnel for directions to the **Churchill Exhibition**. After touring that exhibition, proceed to a guided tour of the State Rooms. Later, you can enjoy Blenheim's Formal and Pleasure Gardens.

Blenheim Palace Lodging Information

Visit the Blenheim Palace website if you're interested in lodging nearby.

Oxford Lodging information is provided in the **Lumos Oxford** section.

Going to Blenheim Palace
🚌 Bussing to Blenheim

S3 Stagecoach Busses to **Blenheim Palace** leave from Oxford Railway Station or Gloucester Green Bus Station several times each hour, beginning at 9:15am. A return ticket will cost less than £6 ($9). Be sure you have **cash** available to pay for your ticket.

Bus schedules *ought to* be available from the bus drivers. But, just in case they aren't, the **Oxford-Blenheim S3 bus schedule** can be found on the Stagecoach Bus website.
http://www.stagecoachbus.com/PdfUploads/Timetable_8898_S3.pdf

The Blenheim S3 bus stop is at the Palace's Hensington Gate. After passing through the ticket gate, it's a 10 to 15 minute walk down the half-mile lane that leads to the large gravel yard in front of the Main Palace entrance.

🚗 Driving to Blenheim

Google Maps UK and SatNav/GPS: Woodstock, Oxfordshire OX20 1PX, UK

[Do *not* use SatNav/GPS address cited by the Blenheim website (Blenheim Palace, Woodstock, Oxfordshire OX20 1PP). Although the gate is well signed, if you follow the Blenheim address coordinates, you could end up far north of the Hensington Gate.]

Enter at Hensington Gate. After buying your ticket (or passing through the gate with a pre-purchased ticket), drive toward the Palace. Watch on your right for the **free Car Park**. From there, it's a 3 to 5 minute walk to the large gravel yard in front of the Main Palace entrance.

All vehicles must be off the premises before 6:30pm, when gates are locked.

30

BODLEIAN LIBRARY

Home of *Two* Harry Potter Places
- The Divinity School: Hogwarts' Infirmary and the *GOF* Dance Practice Room
- Duke Humfrey's Library: Hogwarts' Library

http://www.bodleian.ox.ac.uk/home
http://en.wikipedia.org/wiki/Bodleian_Library

Google Maps UK: Catte St, University of Oxford, Hertford College, Oxford, Oxfordshire OX1, or 51.754121,-1.253943

Travel and lodging information is in the **Lumos Oxford** section.

Visit date restrictions, time requirements, and entry fees information is provided in **Specialis Revelio Oxford**.

Bag Restrictions: Do not bring large bags with you. Visitors must secure all bags, backpacks or purses, in small lockers for the duration of *any* Bodleian tour.

Photography Restrictions: You are welcome to snap Potter Pix within the Divinity School, but *no* pic-taking is permitted within Duke Humfrey's Library.

The Bodleian Library has no public toilet facilities. The nearest non-Potter-Place public toilet is on the south side of **Market Street**, between the **Covered Market** entrance and the **Wagamama** noodle restaurant. (See the **OWLs Map**.)

The Bodleian Libraries are an integrated collection of nearly 40 (yes, *forty*) libraries located in buildings scattered throughout the city of Oxford. As impressive as that sounds, the Bodleian Libraries represent less than half of the *100* Oxford University Libraries (**OULs**).

When spoken of in the *singular*, the **Bodleian Library** refers to five buildings found at the intersection of Broad and Catte streets—also known as the **Central Bodleian Site**. Pronounced "BOD-lee-an," Oxford scholars call it **the Bodley**, or simply **the Bod**. Since we're not Oxford scholars, we call it **the Bodleian**.

The Bodleian is one of the oldest libraries in all of Europe. Containing 120 *miles* of occupied shelving and at least 29 reading rooms, the Bodleian is Britain's second-largest library. (The **British Library** in London is the largest.)

The Bodleian is unique in that it operates principally as a **reference library**—*not* a **lending library**. No one is allowed to remove books or documents from the Bodleian. Legend has it that even King Charles I was refused permission to borrow a book from the Bodleian in 1645. Bodleian Library documents and books may be perused only within a Bodleian reading room.

Reading room access is strictly reserved for students and staff members who have *signed a contract* that legally requires them to honor all Bodleian Library (and OUL) rules. Visitors are only allowed into select reading rooms, and only when guided there by official Bodleian tour personnel.

The two Bodleian Library Potter Places—**Duke Humfrey's Library** and the **Divinity School**—are located within one building of what is known as the **Old Bodleian Library**, an interconnected collection of buildings found just south of Broad Street and west of Catte Street, surrounding the **Old Schools Quadrangle**.

The Bodleian Great Gate
Point A on the Oxford Wizarding Locations Map

[©2011 Tara Bellers] [©2004 Kaihsu Tai]

Although several entrances to the Old Bodleian buildings are available for staff and students, visitors must enter via the **Great Gate** on **Catte Street**, which opens onto the Old Schools Quadrangle. Directly across from the Great Gate, on the west side of the Quadrangle, is the building that houses Duke Humfrey's Library and the Divinity School. Its entrance is guarded by a large bronze statue of **William Herbert**, Third Earl of Pembroke, who was Chancellor of Oxford University from 1617 to 1630.

The Bodleian Tour Ticket Office

[©2011 Tara Bellers]

As you pass through the Great Gate, look to your right and you'll see a **Wooden Lodge**. Bodleian Staff are available here year-round to answer questions, give directions, and sell tickets for each day's Bodleian tours. Apart from Christmas, New Years, and Easter holidays, **the** Bodleian **Wooden Lodge ticket office opens at 9am on Mondays through Saturdays, and at 11am on Sundays.**

The Bodleian Shop
http://www.bodleianshop.co.uk/

Since you cannot take photos within Duke Humfrey's Library, be sure to visit the Bodleian Shop before or after your tour to purchase Duke Humfrey's Library postcards. On the cover of the **Bodleian Library Oxford** guidebook (by Geoffrey Tyack, available in 2008) is a photo of the *Sorcerer's Stone* **Hogwarts Library Restricted Section**.

The shop's entrance is within the Old Schools Quadrangle. Apart from Christmas, New Years, and Easter holidays, the Bodleian Shop is open all year: Monday to Friday from 9am to 5pm, on Saturdays from 9am to 4:30pm, on Sundays from 11am to 5pm.

Unfortunately, there are no official Harry Potter souvenirs for sale in the Bodleian Shop.

Divinity School: Hogwarts Infirmary & Dance Lessons
http://en.wikipedia.org/wiki/Divinity_School,_Oxford

[©2009 Tara Bellers]

The Divinity School is a spectacularly ornate medieval building originally planned as a single-storied structure similar in scope and grandeur to a free-standing chapel. Specifically intended for theology lectures and discussions, the Divinity School is the oldest surviving *purpose-built* Oxford University building. Its foundations were laid in 1424. Unfortunately, Divinity School construction was plagued by frequent financial delays, resulting in several modifications (down-sizing) of the original architectural design over the years. One cannot help but wonder how much *more* grandly ornate the original Divinity School design must have been!

Divinity School Potter Pix

Below are five of our favorite Harry Potter screenshots that show sections of the Divinity School room you'll be able to photograph during your visit.

[*Sorcerer's Stone* screenshot (enhanced)]

The Divinity School's windows were left as they appear in real-life during filming of the *Sorcerer's Stone* infirmary and *Goblet of Fire* dance lesson scenes.

[*Goblet of Fire* screenshot (enhanced)]

[*Chamber of Secrets* screenshot (enhanced)]

But, for *Chamber of Secrets*, *Prisoner of Azkaban*, and *Half-Blood Prince*, CGI Wizards (or Hogwarts Infirmary set designers) altered the Divinity School windows, making their leaded sections diamond-shaped and adding extra architectural embellishments.

[*Prisoner of Azkaban* screenshot (enhanced)]

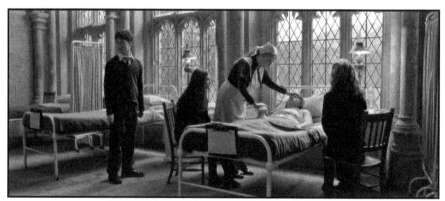

[*Half-Blood Prince* screenshot (enhanced)]

Duke Humfrey's Library: Hogwarts Library
http://en.wikipedia.org/wiki/Duke_Humfrey%27s_Library

The first Oxford University **library** established *apart from* the Oxford Colleges was housed in a room above the **Old Congregation House**, which was erected on a site north of the University Church of St Mary the Virgin. The building stood at the heart of Oxford's academic quarter, close to the schools in which lectures were given. It was built in 1320 with funds supplied by Thomas de Cobham, Bishop of Worcester, but remained unfinished when he died in 1327. This room still exists as a vestry and meeting room, but is neither large nor architecturally impressive.

The construction of a new library was prompted by a deathbed gift to the University in 1447 from **Humfrey, Duke of Gloucester**, the younger brother of King Henry V. Humfrey's gift was his collection of more than 281 priceless and rare, historic manuscripts, including several important classical texts. Because the Old Congregation Library would have been desperately overcrowded by this donation, the University decided to erect a new library *above* the unfinished Divinity School to house Duke Humfrey's books. Plagued with the same funding shortages as the Divinity School, construction of Duke Humfrey's Library wasn't completed until 1488.

Sadly, Humphrey's impressive collection did not survive to present day. During the Reformation of 1550, the Crown removed all books from Duke Humphrey's library in a vain attempt to destroy the vestiges of Roman Catholicism. Humphrey's books were likely burned. Today only three of the original books belonging to Duke Humfrey remain in the collection.
http://atlasobscura.com/place/duke-humphrey-s-library-at-the-old-bodleian-library

Duke Humfrey's Library Potter Site Rating

 vs vs

After going through all the trouble of obtaining access to this OWL (see **Specialis Revelio Oxford**), you'll **not be allowed to take Potter Pix** within Duke Humfrey's Library—even with your mobile phone! Similarly difficult-to-reach *Harry Potter Places*, especially those where photography is prohibited, commonly receive a **Might-Be-Fun**, or even a **Skip It** rating.

Duke Humfrey's Library retains a **Great Site** rating in spite of these difficulties and limitations, because Potterites who reach it will be **walking** *within* **Hogwarts Library**. Very little was altered or augmented when Harry Potter scenes were filmed here. The short YouTube video link below will give you a sense of why Duke Humfrey's Library is such a great site to visit.
http://www.youtube.com/watch?v=JgyqZXMLMdM

Duke Humfrey's Library Potter Screenshots

During your tour, keep your eyes on the *windows* in order to recognize places where Harry Potter filming took place. Our first four Duke Humfrey's Library screenshots demonstrate the windows you should be watching for.

[*Sorcerer's Stone* screenshots (enhanced) above and below]

[*Chamber of Secrets* screenshot (enhanced)]

[*Half-Blood Prince* screenshot (enhanced)]

Throughout your tour, be especially vigilant for the **Hogwarts Library Restricted Section** seen in *Sorcerer's Stone*.

[*Sorcerer's Stone* screenshot (enhanced)]

To recognize this location, watch for the wooden pillars and gate guarding this special collection of Bodleian Library books.

[Bodleian Guidebook Cover Scan, ©2005 Geoffrey Tyack]

Duke Humfrey's Library images can be purchased in the Bodleian Shop.

31

Christ Church College

Hogwarts Great Hall and Grand Stairway
http://www.chch.ox.ac.uk/
http://en.wikipedia.org/wiki/Christ_Church,_Oxford
http://www.chch.ox.ac.uk/visiting/harry-potter

Google Maps UK: Saint Aldates, Oxford, OX1 1 (Christ Church)

Travel and lodging information is in the **Lumos Oxford** section.

Operation Hours: Mon-Sat 9am to 5pm, Sunday 2pm to 5pm. Closed on Christmas Day and Good Friday. The Dining Hall (Hogwarts Great Hall) is closed daily from 11:45am to 2:15 pm, so that students can eat lunch.

Entry Fee: Adults £8 ($12); Children, Seniors, Students with ID, £6.50 ($10); Children under 5 admitted free. Admission includes an illustrated Christ Church College and Cathedral pamphlet.

Cathedral Shop Hours: Mon-Sat, 10am to 5pm; Sunday, noon to 5pm

Visit Time: Schedule at least 90 minutes here.

Parseltongue Pointer:
- Frideswide = "FRIDES-wide" (like "BRIDES-wide")

C380

Christ Church College is the thirteenth of the present-day Oxford colleges to be founded, but the ground it occupies was a place of Christian worship and education long before then. Near the end of the 7th Century, a Saxon noblewoman named **Frideswide** founded a nunnery here in order to escape the attentions of an Anglo-Saxon prince who wanted her to renounce her celibacy vow and become his wife. During the years she spent avoiding abduction to remain a nun, Frideswide performed several healing miracles and was considered a Saint by those in Oxfordshire. **Saint Frideswide's Parish church** was established on this site long before her official canonization in 1480.

Today, Frideswide is the **Patron Saint of Oxford**. Her feast day is October 19th. Her shrine is located in **Christ Church Cathedral**, where her image can be seen in medieval as well as Pre-Raphaelite stained glass.

During the Danish massacre ordered by King Ethelred II in 1002, Saint Frideswide's Parish Church was burned to the ground then rebuilt. An **Augustinian Priory** was established there during the reign of Henry I (1122), which came to be known as **Saint Frideswide's Monastery**. In 1524, with the support of King Henry VIII, Cardinal Wolsey dissolved the monastery and usurped its buildings so that he could found **Cardinal's College**. After Wolsey's fall from power, Henry re-founded the College in 1546, christening the old monastery church as the **Christ Church Cathedral of the new Diocese of Oxford**.

Since that time, Christ Church College has produced *thirteen* **British prime ministers**, which is equal to the combined number produced by all 45 of the other Oxford colleges.

The Christ Church College Visitor Entrance

[©2009 Tara Bellers]

Point B on the **Oxford Wizarding Locations Map** identifies the main visitor entrance on the south side of Christ Church College: a large stone arch opening in the middle of the **Meadow Building**, aptly called **Meadow Gate**. The free pamphlet you'll receive upon paying for admission provides a map as well as step-by-step directions for touring the College and Cathedral from this point. Similarly, our Potter Pix directions begin at the Meadow Gate entrance.

Wheelchair access to Christ Church College is via the **Tom Gate** beneath **Tom Tower**, on **Saint Aldate's** (street)—identified on the OWLs Map as a circled **T**.

Please Note: If the Meadow Gate entrance queue is exceptionally long, walk back to Saint Aldate's, turn right and walk north to enter via the Tom Gate. Long lines are rarely found at Tom Gate—or Canterbury Gate on Oriel Square. After paying for admission at one of these entrances, use the Christ Church pamphlet map to find your way to the shop and follow Potter Pix directions.

The Christ Church Cathedral Shop

Not all Potter Places with shops pay for a license to sell Harry Potter items. The Cathedral Shop *is* licensed, and sells all sorts of Potter souvenirs: books, key chains, action figures, pin badges, coffee mugs—even Tom Riddle's Diary. Be sure to allow ample time to enjoy the shop during your visit.

The Most Iconic HP Places Are at Christ Church College

[*Chamber of Secrets* Ultimate Edition screenshot (enhanced)]

Seen in all eight Harry Potter movies, the original **Hogwarts Great Hall set** design was based on the Tudor architecture of the grand **Dining Hall** in Christ Church College.

[©2009 Tara Bellers]

Anticipating that it would be used for many years of filming, Hogwarts Great Hall was constructed with a solid stone floor, exceptionally thick walls, and populated with hardwood tables and benches—all of which constituted an enormous expense and a degree of permanence quite unusual for film set construction. Now that the movies are finished, this set has been preserved and moved to the **Harry Potter WB Studio Tour (Site #27)**, a London Side-Along Apparation.

Contrary to what some might tell you, no filming ever took place within the Dining Hall. However, two other areas of Christ Church College *were* **location film sites** for *Sorcerer's Stone* and *Chamber of Secrets* scenes.

Please Note: Christ Church College is so familiar looking, be sure to take turns being your group's photographer. Send your companions ahead to pose while you snap shots with **everyone's cameras**. Then switch. Because both photographers shoot 2 or 3 pix with each camera, it will rarely take more than two sessions at each site to capture screenshot reproduction pix that include *everyone*.

Christ Church Potter Pix Directions

Enter Christ Church College from the Meadow Gate and follow signs to the **Cathedral Shop**. When you reach the shop entrance, walk *past* it, watching on your right for an elevated alcove containing two windows, above a plaque memorializing, "Jeremy Angus Sebastian Clement Kitchen."

[©2011 Tara Bellers]

For *Sorcerer's Stone* filming, this plaque was covered by the display case set piece that contained **James Potter's Quidditch Trophy**. Walk a few steps beyond the plaque, turn around, and snap your first Potter Pix.

Christ Church Potter Pic #1

[*Sorcerer's Stone* screenshot (enhanced)]

[©2011 Tara Bellers]

As you can see in Tara's pic above, the real-life background in your photos will look exactly like the screenshot's background.

When finished, head back the way you came, watching on your right for the hallway that leads into the tower containing the **Grand Stairway** to the **Dining Hall**. When you reach the stairway, back up far enough to snap the next Potter Pic: Harry looking on from below, as Hermione and Ron chat on the landing in front of the Dining Hall.

Christ Church Potter Pic #2

[*Sorcerer's Stone* screenshot (enhanced)]

Only the Hog Statue seen in this screenshot was a set piece. All else, including the lamp posts, exist in real life. The pic-taker should crouch low to the ground so that the amazing, fan-traceried, vaulted ceiling is captured in each photo.

Next, look to your left. For *Chamber of Secrets*, Harry and Ron were filmed racing up this short flight of steps after being ejected from the Flying Ford Anglia. A green screen was erected behind the arched entryway so that a background plate of Hogwarts Lake could be inserted.

Christ Church Potter Pic #3

[*Chamber of Secrets* screenshot (enhanced)]

Obviously, there'll not be stacks of trunks and magical creatures' cages—nor a flaming pedestal or Hog Statue—in view. But, no one will fail to recognize the photos you take of this film site.

The next two screenshots are accomplished from the same general location, with your character stand-ins ascending the first section of the Grand Stairway.

Christ Church Potter Pic #4

[*Chamber of Secrets* screenshot (enhanced)]

Above, Harry and Ron reach the first Grand Stairway landing as they continue their dash to the Dining Hall. Below is the scene where Harry first sees Tom Riddle after being sucked into his diary.

[*Chamber of Secrets* screenshot (enhanced)]

After snapping these pix, walk up to the first Grand Stairway landing, round the corner, and send your Professor-McGonagall-stand-in up to the landing in front of the Dining Hall entrance so that you can take pix of her/him greeting First-Year Students. If you manage to include the carved features above the Dining Hall's door in your shots, you'll be able to recreate both of the screenshots below in one set of pix.

Christ Church Potter Pic #5

[*Sorcerer's Stone* screenshots (enhanced) above and below]

The next Potter Pic is super fun, especially since you'll look terrifically silly while taking it! Crouch as low as you can on a step just below the Dining Hall landing and have your Professor-McGonagall-stand-in lean over you. It may work best if you lay on your back with your head on the last step before the landing.

Christ Church Potter Pic #6

[*Sorcerer's Stone* screenshot (enhanced)]

You're a tourist! Who cares if you look silly while snapping pix? To be fair, each member of your party should be given the opportunity to have her/his pic snapped from this angle.

Please Note: During times of high visitor traffic, polite Potterites will patiently wait for a lull in the flow, rather than blocking the stairs. If a lull is not forthcoming, move to the very center of the staircase (where the white tiles provide a division for traffic direction), allowing others to continue up or down the steps on either side of you while quickly shooting your pix.

Christ Church Potter Pic #7

After you reach the Dining Hall's landing, turn around and capture pix of a McGonagall-stand-in's *back*, as she/he looks down the Grand Stairway's final flight at approaching First-Year Students.

[*Sorcerer's Stone* screenshot (enhanced)]

Christ Church Potter Pic #8

While still on the Dining Hall landing, have your McGonagall-stand-in step aside so that you can shoot pix of Harry and Ron (or other visitors) reaching the first landing in *Chamber of Secrets*. Scenes of Harry following Tom Riddle while Dumbledore looked on were also shot from this vantage point.

[*Chamber of Secrets* screenshots (enhanced) above and below]

Christ Church Potter Pic #9

Next, lean over the Dining Hall landing's upper railing to look down and snap pix of First-Year Students (other visitors) heading to the area at the base of the Grand Stairway.

[*Sorcerer's Stone* screenshot (enhanced)]

Christ Church Potter Pic #10

Enter the Christ Church College Tudor Dining Hall to snap Hogwarts Great Hall pix.

[*Chamber of Secrets* screenshot (enhanced)]

Christ Church Potter Pic #11

Be sure to take a few pix while facing back toward the door you entered.

[*Chamber of Secrets* screenshot (enhanced)]

Although the door won't be closed during your visit, Photoshop savvy Potterites can import a closed door when they return home from holiday.

After capturing your Potter Pix, visit the Cathedral Shop. If you have loads of time after that, enjoy the many splendid non-Potter parts of Christ Church College and Cathedral. The pamphlet you will be given contains a good deal of non-Potter information. Potterites interested in more information can purchase the *Christ Church Guidebook* that has only recently become available.

When finished at Christ Church, it's faster to reach the next OWL (or the bus station) by leaving via the **Canterbury Gate: Point C** on the **OWLs Map**. This exit is found near the **Picture Gallery**, which is clearly identified on the Christ Church pamphlet's map.

32

NEW COLLEGE

Goblet of Fire Scenes
http://www.new.ox.ac.uk/
http://en.wikipedia.org/wiki/New_College,_Oxford

Google Maps UK: 8 New College Lane, Oxford OX1
(Winter Entrance: 1-20 Holywell St, Oxford, OX1 3)

Travel and lodging information is in the **Lumos Oxford** section.

Operation Hours & Entry fee: See below.

Visit Time: 30 to 45 minutes here should be plenty, unless you're also interested in touring the non-Potter parts.

Parseltongue Pointer:
• Wykeham = "WICK-um"

CB80

Despite its name, **New College** is one of the oldest Oxford colleges, having been founded in 1379 by **William of Wykeham**, who was Bishop of Winchester and High Chancellor during the reign of **King Edward III**. Although primarily established for the education of priests, lay persons were also schooled at New College. The Wikipedia link above offers a marvelously condensed account of New College's history, descriptions of its architecture, and a list of notable alumni.

Another of Wykeham's primary purposes for founding New College was rather selfish, yet destined to earn international acclaim for the college. Bishop Wykeham ordained the creation of a choir of sixteen boys and young clerics charged with singing mass for the repose of his soul at his death, and *forever* after. Today, the **New College Choir** is known as one of the finest Anglican choirs in the world. The choir tours internationally and has recorded more than seventy albums—two of which have earned **Gramophone Awards**.
http://www.newcollegechoir.com

During each school term there is a full **Choral Evensong** service at 6:15pm on Saturdays and on every weekday evening (except for Wednesdays). Sunday's Choral Evensong is at 6pm. To obtain a *taste* of what a New College Choral Evensong sounds like, visit the choir's collection of services broadcast on the Internet.
http://www.newcollegechoir.com/webcast-archive.html

If overnighting in Oxford, consider returning to New College in time to enjoy hearing these fantastic voices within New College's magnificent chapel. There is no fee for attending the service. Donations are used to support the Chapel's charities.

In 1400, the New College **Cloisters** and **Bell Tower** were the last parts of the original buildings to be completed. The Cloisters are a covered outdoor walk surrounding a grass quadrangle. Here is where several *Harry Potter and the Goblet of Fire* scenes were filmed in 2004.

In the northwest corner of the Cloisters' grass quadrangle lives a nineteenth-century *Quercus Ilex*—an evergreen **Holm Oak** (aka **Holly Oak**). Beneath the boughs of this great tree is the area where Mad-Eye Moody turned Draco Malfoy into a white ferret. Scenes immediately preceding that event were shot within the Cloisters.

Although the footage easily recognized as having been filmed here doesn't fill a great deal of screen time, New College Porters report that it took 3 weeks to accomplish *GOF* filming. We suspect that several Hogwarts hallways scenes were also shot within the Cloisters.

When you visit, please keep in mind that the Cloisters is a place dedicated to peace and quiet, meditation and study. Polite Potterites will invoke the **Quietus Spell**, or activate a **Silencio Charm**.

Operation Hours & Entry fees: Mid-March to Mid-October

The **New College Lane** entrance to New College and its Cloisters is open every day of the week from 11am to 4:45pm during the bulk of the year.

A £2 ($3) entry fee is charged for adults. Children, Seniors, and Students with valid IDs are charged £1.50 ($2). Bodleian card holders, Oxford Alumni, and residents of Oxford are admitted free.

Operation Hours & Entry fees: Mid-October to Mid-March

During winter months, New College must be accessed from the **Holywell Street** entrance. Open only from 2pm to 4pm each day, there is no entry fee.

Unfortunately, a multi-page, glossy **New College Guidebook** (a souvenir divinely desired) does *not* exist—likely because **New College has no shop**. Upon paying your admission fee, you'll be given a 1-page map and a 2-page

Tourist Leaflet—items that can be downloaded from the Internet prior to your visit.

http://www.new.ox.ac.uk/system/files/College_Map_0.pdf
http://www.new.ox.ac.uk/system/files/Tourist%20Leaflet.pdf

A public toilet *is* available within New College. Ask for directions to the **Long Room** building, south of the **Main Garden Quad**.

No photography is allowed inside any New College *buildings*, including the amazing medieval Chapel. Happily, photography *is* allowed within the Cloisters and its grassy quadrangle—the Harry Potter Places.

New College Cloisters Potter Pix

Because only *Goblet of Fire* scenes were filmed here, we'll forgo captioning each of the enhanced screenshots below.

After entering New College from **New College Lane** and paying admission at the **Old Porter's Lodge**, you'll arrive at the **Front Quadrangle**. Turn left and walk a few steps north, looking left for the entrance to the **New College Cloisters**.

New College Cloisters Potter Pic #1

The **south Cloisters walk** is just beyond the Cloisters entrance. This is where Harry was filmed while winding his way through scores of students sporting *"Potter Stinks!"* and *"Support Cedric Diggory!"* button-pins.

New College Cloisters Potter Pic #2

After reaching the **east Cloisters walk** (the section that leads to the right from the entrance), Harry enters the Cloisters' grass quadrangle. The northeast corner is seen in the background.

New College Cloisters Potter Pic #3

After passing an iron astronomy statue (a *set piece* that doesn't exist in real-life), Harry finds Cedric Diggory sitting with several chums and draws him aside to tell him that the first Tri-Wizard Challenge involves dragons. Along with branches of the Holm Oak seen behind Cedric, the northeast corner of New College Cloisters is seen in the background.

The remaining scenes all involve the great Holm Oak found in the northwest corner of the Cloisters' quadrangle.

New College Cloisters Potter Pic #4

Although Malfoy is first seen sitting *within* the tree's branches, please **do *not* climb on the great Holm Oak.** Instead, have pix taken while you and other members of your party are standing beside its trunk.

New College Cloisters Potter Pic #5

The infamous scenes of Mad-Eye making Malfoy-the-Ferret dance in the air—much to the chagrin of Professor McGonagall—were shot beneath the great Holm Oak.

New College Cloisters Potter Pic #6

If you're collecting photos of the *traceried openings* found at various UK Cloisters where Harry Potter filming took place, beneath the Holm Oak is a great place to capture pix of the New College Cloisters' arches.

[©2009 Tara Bellers]

After snapping your New College Cloisters Potter Pix, you can explore the non-Potter parts of New College. However, if you leave this site earlier than the time allotted during our suggested itineraries, you'll have more time to spend at your *next* OWL—one with a shop.

THE END

Thus ends the adventures of
Harry Potter Places Book Two ...

Please join us in Harry Potter Places
Book Three—Snitch Seeking in
Southern England and Wales

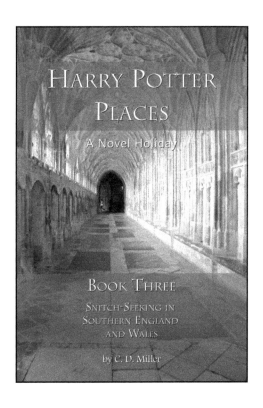

INDEX